Looking INWARDS

A Journey into Turiya

SAMEER PENDSE

notionpress.com

INDIA • SINGAPORE • MALAYSIA

ISBN 979-8-89002-905-8

Contents

PART II – MIDDLE YEARS IN INDIA

PART III – STARTING IN THE UK

Prologue—An Essay—Poetry and Society

The answers to questions such as, "Why does consciousness exist?", "What is the purpose of our life?", and "Is there a divinity?" are more relevant to theology (Sanatana Dharma, Vedanta) and philosophy (Existentialism). Psychoanalysts get into the theory of dreams and talk about them as sublime and abstract means of conveying deeper and hidden thought processes of the mind (even spirituality can be seen as a mode of thinking) and eventually as a means to bring peace to the mind of the afflicted. Poetry can be seen as complementary to these, a tool for introspection, a means for artistic satisfaction and lastly, a unique way of looking at reality, which makes awareness a heightened and beatific experience.

The poet does not in any way strive to be a willful educator or proponent of any particular school of thought. Poetry is a form of self-expression in the same way our existence is considered a form of expression. Now that we are here and short of putting an end to this cause (we don't know for sure what happens after the light goes out), we might as well enjoy the pleasure of exploring the hidden depths of our minds and hence our talents. From our first feeble attempts at creating and constructing, piece by piece, we eventually come to appreciate and thrill at our efforts in juxtaposing people, places, memories, pains, and pleasures into some framework, which gives us a sense of euphoria and general well-being that makes us thankful to be alive and kicking.

It seems to be a common understanding in the collective consciousness of mankind that pain is what stimulates us into action. A happy man, content whether spiritually, materially, or sexually, is rarely stimulated into exploring the depths of his psyche. Writing about bitter moments, and moments of humiliation and hurt do lead to a catharsis, and with it comes an openness to lateral thinking and resolution, i.e., philosophical discussions with the self about the whys and wherefores of corporeal being. To quote from my award-winning poem, "Forgiving Yourself":

"Accepting fate, accepting that some moments in life will never return

Thinking is futile—forgiving yourself for your inadequacies,

Writing and getting it out of your head—in poetry,

Striving for balance, between logic, meta-logic, and emotion."

With experience comes the realization that people respond to poetry, as it influences their lives and hence self-evolution leads to the progress of collective consciousness. It is at this point that poetry becomes a social responsibility in the same way that judicial or military systems are. There is little to be said about a culture that can keep its peace but can enjoy the higher pleasures of the mind. To quote from one of my poems, "Free Association":

"Pain breaks the shackles, makes for a sensitive mind

The start of the journey towards enlightened sight

Feel it, abide it, trust it, and write it

Share the knowledge life has wrought, contribute to the creative might

By contemplating the way of all life with fellow sentient forms

Enriching life experiences—not good intentions but good results

Bring on the suffering so may come forth the greatness of mankind."

Poets are thought leaders of mankind. Spirituality, history, heritage, and romance, even empathy, is the legacy we leave behind, as we are buffeted by the cruel tides of fortune. Penury, hunger, persecution, social castigation, and familial opinions have never dimmed the poetic heart and never will. Upholding the social fabric and keeping the flame of social conscience burning is a necessity that all writers of verse eventually realize. Commercial art and sport eventually turn populist, as the human mind tends to succumb to cheap thrill and lethargy rather than exert itself towards a higher and subtler pleasure of appreciation. More so now than ever, do the popular mediums induce the dope-filled stupor needed to keep sedated the teeming multitude of destitute and under-privileged humans—these being in number far greater than the discriminating audience. Eventually, the commercial economics are skewed in favor of what the masses adore, rather than that which would lead to a finer sense of understanding about the human condition.

Lest we get lost in the pedantic ramblings of knowledge and resistance against social ills and dogmas, there is a more mundane, and in the final analysis, more warm purpose that poetry serves. It keeps us loving and calm, and that in itself seems to be a necessary and sufficient pre-condition (& post-condition) to life. From a song of mine, "Abstract Love":

"Life without love, a hell without hope

Brilliance without heart, getting old and cold

Love without a name

Without religion

Without condition,

An inner joy

A God it would be."

I hope we do not subject love to the same scrutiny to which divinity is submitted, for it is tacit that love is that singular feeling, which brings us energy, hope, good cheer, and happiness. And so, I summarize with a verse from my poem, "Illusion Revisited Today":

"The realization of the deepest realization of loss, love

And finally, the value of, the beauty of love that passes possessing

Beyond the pure consciousness of the supreme void,

The translucent yellowish flakes of soft white love that emanate

From a divine being that does have a form."

The greatest mission we have as poets in society is to keep love alive—for, from love comes the glue, the antidote, and the cure for all of life's common maladies, keeping us all together in peace. In saying that, does poetry not serve as the gasoline that keeps us human beings running, though it is the nature of society today that we believe that it is science, commerce, and agriculture that are the reasons for social status and wealth being our measures of worth and success and eventually happiness?

PART I – IN AMERICA

Looking Inwards

Looking inwards for reason…
For love,
For faith,
For patience,
For light,
For consciousness,
For life, death, and rebirth,
For suffering,
For relationships.

Realizing after much introspection, meditation, devotion, and service
That the answer is a state of grace
From the Gurus and from God.
Illumination is a state of grace;
It can't be forced,
It can't be craved,
It can't be begged,
It can't be demanded;
It has to be completely detached.
The final light
Is an answer to all answers.

To Be and Not to Be

There is a distinct dichotomy that is readily preached
Either living in the real world and embracing all its callings
Or living in the spiritual world renouncing all its ills.
But there has to be middle ground;
Otherwise, why would the maker have created
Both the conflicting halves of one hell of a merry-go-round?

Reality is very real;
Every blow or modicum of happiness can be undeniably felt.
There is no point in contemplating an escape,
As one would land up here again.
But after another long transitional cycle,
There was a point of the material world;
"Not a random illusion perpetuated to bewitch us."
That is what he says, and that is what we should reflect on.

To traverse into alternate existence is tempting beyond reasoning.
To be free of pain, suffering, desire, angst, and some moments of bliss;
To experience an eternal satisfaction and contentment beyond imagination.
But he reiterates—anything forced, anything you are not born into,
Is not a destination of any lasting sort.

So that brings us to the middle ground;
Be a part of what our senses perceive as real

Along with its seemingly pointless purposes
While living a detached life of the seeker as you step out of the door
Into a world which is yours and yours alone—one where you are not being.

The good of each realm can feed into the other.
From one you learn the power of creativity, discipline,
Focus, and making concrete plans
From the other, the value of love, welfare, serenity, and
Selfless commitment in whatever you endeavor to undertake.

That seems about right—marrying both conflicting halves.
What was meant to be, will be.
What exists is with purpose, including all that we can see and can't.
We do what we need to,
All in keeping with the plans of the benevolent supramental.
Believe, unabashedly and unreservedly.

Where Do We Land?

Death is not the end nor a fresh beginning –
It is somewhere in between.
A start but with what we carry forward,
And part blessings of the higher order.
So, as we come to the end of this life or the contemplation of it,
We are left thinking, "What next?"

After we have run through life's desires,
Some of us might have gained a level of comfort;
But most of us are ploughing through a tortured existence,
With some interim respite.
Where do we land in the future
And what and who do we gather around
as our nears and dears in a new birth?

Sure, it's a renewal: a new body and an enhanced soul with veiled memories;
But it is a movement leaving our comfort zones behind.
For some, a chance for a better situation and simpler circumstances.
Maybe moving into better environments after the despair of
Poverty, loneliness, disease, and a multitude of disasters.

It can bring real anxiety and terror,
Thinking where we might land or end up.
Not just thinking of the future of this life

But the next and what it might be.
Faith is the key to the burgeoning fear;
The almighty and emissaries working hand-in-hand
To assure for you, a better future.

So, believe that we will be blessed with enough love;
Believe that we will be protected from malevolent forces;
Believe that circumstances will be provided for accelerated spiritual development;
And there will be no dearth of food, clothing, and shelter.

Only faith can get us by.
We try to control this life but the real challenge is the after-life.
Faith and worship are the key;
Losing ourselves in prayers of divine intervention
Immersing in the energy that binds us all
As our visions extend gradually to eternity.
Believing that all will be well when we land
After this particular voyage on rough seas.

Hazardous Waste

It was a memorable evening
Of festivities, good music, and renewed acquaintances.
And while we drank our red wines and partook of idle bantering,
The erudite nurse and her words kept coming to mind in the backdrop:
"You guys only have prostates and cholesterol to deal with;
We got hormonal, cervical, breast, ovarian,
Osteoporosis, knees, and pregnancies to contend with."
And that got me thinking:
While reflecting on the messages from the mother,
The real hazardous waste is our mindset about women
And the objectification we bring
To their very existence in everyday life.

Everyone has a right to live the way they want;
Appear the way they choose;
Study what they like;
And opt for a profession or sport of their own predilection.
Everyone has the right to love whoever they want
And ignore whoever they don't.
Freedom of expression is everyone's birthright
And especially for our mothers, sisters, and friends too.

Everyone needs breathing space in life;
As if it is not enough to suffer through a monthly ordeal.

Contend with being pursued through looks and comments in all perceivable ways,

To be forever conscious of where to walk, sit, exist, and still too by the time of day.

The real hazardous waste is in our attitudes
As fathers, brothers, bosses, and friends.
Some have it right, some have it quite wrong.
You can't wage wars over who owns whom.

We live in a rapidly evolving world
And it is time to let go, to let them be.
Admire if you want, but do it from a distance
And not tainted by illusionary hurt or denial.
They are the true core of a stable society;
And the more we accept that,
The more the twains will prosper as a whole.

Bullets & Bombs

What we have done is an abomination;
And what we do in the future
Will not be enough by any yardstick.
Mother nature has her own bullets and bombs,
To bring order back onto this planet we call civilization.

It all started happening in short measures –
Hurricanes, droughts, floods, the proliferation of pandemics;
Shortage of food, internal wars, diseases due to ozone depletion.
Soon the day will come, when there is suddenly no oxygen to breathe,
Or no food to eat, or no land to live on.
Submerged below the dissolving ice caps,
Soon the day will come;
When the fostering mother will decide to reinvigorate this blessed planet,
For its less fortunate and voiceless inhabitants.

The regional wars just carry on.
For the poor, death and torture.
For the more fortunate, the blasts turn into small spheres of sparkling gold orbs.
A protection from the vagaries of conflict;
But these might come to an end too
As we turn our sectarianism and bigotry into a global situation.

One way out is to learn lessons from the stone age.
Reduce our footprints to be in synch with minimal living;
Bear fewer kids, bear no arms, bear simplicity in our hearts;
Live in peace with our planet, disavow avarice.
Living with bare essentials might sound like socialism once again;
But it's more about allowing future generations to survive without paying the price;
Otherwise, she has the bullets and bombs to put us down like an infestation of rats.

As we let go, complete detachment not unlike that of a monk
Will help us rise above the things that hold us down
And take us closer to the almighty.
Though the fear of separation can be intense,
This ascendancy of the soul and spirit
Will bring us into harmony with what she desires most.

Flowers of Paradise

The calmer you get inside,
The reduced choppiness you feel in the inner sea of tranquility.
The more meditative the state at the bottom of the liquid ocean,
As you spend more time loving,
And lesser and lesser hating and hurting.
In the absence of angst, not necessarily from a repetitive chant
But from an intense intellectual examination that erodes all impediments;
The holy union comes to the seeker.

Adinath and Adi Maya are no longer dichotomies –
They reveal themselves in half-and-half;
An amalgamation of all the values they stand for,
And the creative and transformative forces in our existence.

They promise of a joy that cannot be imagined,
A liberation that is the freest state of mind.
There are no questions left unanswered;
Everything makes sense and doubts clear up.
The Shiva-Shakti communion is so complete,
That the perceiver knows not where one starts and the other ends.

No longer is Adinath the decider of fate and Adi Shakti the transport there;
Rather, they are together in taking you forward with a combined intent.

Beyond religions and distinct paths to get there—there is an intimate relief
That spans a mountain of lifetimes and a plethora of suffering.
The mind sees and resonates with the saffron *Om*
And distinct consciousness ceases to exist.

The flowers of paradise—our next of kin, the next generation
Have a major role to play in our personal evolution.
In absorption of their continuous growth,
In guiding them through travails of what we call life,
Delighting in their innocence and softening the unravelling of it,
Showing them the path to being better beings.
In adoration of their unadulterated appreciation of all things they come across,
Their unwavering zest for turning the pages to new days and nights,
These flowers of paradise bring serenity and fullness
To what would be emptiness otherwise.
A kind of meditation on the real beauty manifested in reality.

The Source of All Things High

It is hard to tell whether partings or loneliness, which is the most painful of all.

Partings lead to loneliness, but it is the separation that hurts like hell.

Whether it is the tear-ridden farewells between a mother and her child,

Whether it is the heartache of the departure of a disciple from the master,

Whether it is the goodbyes of students after spending years together,

Friends and compatriots, those that spent half a lifetime growing up side-by-side,

The chance that each will not see the other ever again.

It can be unbearable, the feeling that settles in, in the afternoon of a distant land

That the parting is forever, never to be united again.

Never to eat and drink together, never to share a smile together,

Never to share a hug and a kiss,

Never to share a scenic setting by falling dusk or by the rising sun,

Never to hang around doing nothing but just being together.

You can spend days in that feeling of loss

Where you lose and lose and sometimes even your very thoughts

Get replaced by a grief that may never materialize.

But it's there in the settling vacuum,

The deepest feeling of losing something and maybe all that's precious.

Then as you lie on a bed by settling evening and fading light,

The source of all things high, the singular point, casts forth the saffron *Aum.*

And in the accompanying white light,

All sentient living things merge, including the divine.

Adinath, Adimaya, the elephants, the tigers, the trees, the smallest of micro-organisms,

Us humans, us non-humans, all the collective love for one and all;

All are united in the all-absorbing light.

This is Advaita, the timeless state of being.

We are all together, we are all united.

We are never parted, as we were always together.

We are one and that is the ultimate truth;

We all came from and will return to the *Aum.*

So that leaves the only question worth answering –

"If we are one, why was our distinct consciousness

Manifested to be in constant suffering?"

Enlightenment

One can spend lifetimes seeking enlightenment,
Seeking a permanent state of *Turiya*.
Communion with one and all and a lasting glimpse of the divine
But it all comes in stages—little steps to the final objective;
Answers to all questions possible
And the special answer to the most elusive of them all –
"Why are we distinctly manifesting consciousnesses in constant unease?"

It helps to recognize the steps in the journey,
To know that you are on the right track to the elusive solution.
If it all comes in one go, you can go mad or end your life;
Better that it comes in settling and gradual steps.

When the serpent fire awakens,
You feel the strongest desire to forgive the self and others.
Then as she ascends,
There come various states of mind with her journey upwards.
As she reaches your heart,
You open your mind to deep compassionate love for all around;
As she reaches your throat,
You experience a renunciation and detachment from all bondings and desires;
A maturity that accepts everything as being the will of God
And a warmth that kindles the fire in all you decide to focus on.

As she reaches the third eye, you begin to see symbols of Adinath –
Blue pearls, white flames, tridents, and bluish white lights.
You also begin to receive subliminal messages
From nirvanic souls and later from the mother herself;
Adinath may talk to you, send heavy messages that can burden the mind
As you strive to reconcile yourself
With the secrets and mysteries of the universe and beyond.

At the pinnacle of the body,
The soul begins to leave the body in full consciousness
And the final six remain.
Not known much but he,
One of the leaders of the Nath line
Did mention some detail.
As we reach the final phase of the journey,
The ultimate opens itself to us
And reveals the coveted mystery,
The secret of creation and existence—the *Aum*.

You can't scream from rooftops,
What these experiences mean to you.
But *Turiya* is its own reward and once you have it,
You will know how precious it is.
Well worth all the fear, the bleeding, the palpitations,
And the headaches you might experience.
The final contentment that is more a blessing,
Than an aspiration that you craved for
Since the beginning of yourself.

Stone Age

Sometimes I feel like going back to the stone ages,
When we didn't chase riches like nobody's business
But just fulfilled the ultimate objective
Which is a communion with God Almighty.

Why chase fashion or beautiful clothes or tasty food?
Hunt and grow only what you need;
Exchange it with each other for goods
And return back to a barter economy.

The skies are clean
And the Milky Way shines bright at night.
Enjoy each other as images of God.
Why do you need to work beyond tilling the soil,
When thinking can be immersed in the divine?

Was the caveman happier than us during his time?
I sometimes think so.
No running around for lucre or fame or fortune,
When all you have is within you.
Just protect and preserve what you need
For tending to the family.

The only catcher in the rye is –
"How do you run a healthcare system with no money?"
Life expectancy will be so much shorter in this alternate reality.
But on the other hand, what did we achieve with our longer lives?
Just accumulating possessions rather than the love that takes us high.

I hate thinking nowadays.
When you can be in *Turiya*, why settle for innovative dialogues?
When you can be in silence, why invest words to twist the mind further?
Let's all get there with lots of meditation and commitment to each other,
Rather than pointless objectives.

The Daughter We Never Had

I first fell in love with a beating heart on a sonographic display;
Then we were left heartbroken when he/she didn't come out sound.
Our boys have more than made up for the hurt
But we still occasionally wonder whether it was a daughter we never had.

As one door closes, many others open;
It's a matter of points of view and perception.
Call her by a name, drawing pictures,
Or call her by any other name, scribbling on walls.
Call her by many names, playing soccer with a dimpled smile,
We found daughters more than one for the one we never had.

While love is love, whether for a son or for a daughter,
There is something different to be expected in each case.
And that makes for the allure, mystery, and charm,
As daughters play with a doll collection,
Or pamper a pet obtained after much demand.

You come to realize that they care deeply for our frowns and fancies,
Whether helping with cooking a dish or loading the washing machine;
Whether playing a melodic tune on the piano;
Or studying late at night over a book review.

They are different in the clothes they prefer,
And in how easily they can be moved to tears.
They will be different for the careers they will pursue,
Or the family they choose.
But one thing you can always count on is –
They will never let you down in temper as sometimes a son can do.

So, love is love whether for a girl or a boy
But they handle the emotional stress better
While juggling through several tasks at once.
And while strength is strength, they have an edge if given the chance
To be the nucleus of society,
Supporting breadwinners or being breadwinners themselves.

Random Musings

The fans had more fun than the superstar.
While they celebrated, the fellow idols commiserated.
They can't get out, they know no other life.
Their circle, their mates, their friends,
All sealed in place by their walk of life.
And the peer pressure!
The money is like honey for the circling parasites;
They need to keep running to maintain the needed lifestyle.
The limelight is so fickle, fortunes of men flicker by its uncertain light.

Can you say you are alive, if you don't feel the passage of time?
Can you claim to be alive, if you don't feel the suffering of fellow men?
We will all be old eventually, with one foot in the grave.
Find your maker and make peace with all your demons
Before the sunset comes into play.

Regulate, regulate, regulate before it is too late;
Government has a chance to keep the balance in check.
Technology can be boon in saving human life,
And a bane that will claim our lives otherwise.

She reads it and says, "Amen to that!"
So the musings are not without merit,
I come to realize.

Maine

I had always been a Europhile,
Gushing over the lakes of Zurich and Geneva,
The long winding parks of Windsor,
The Lochs of Scotland and the snow of Zermatt,
The cobbled by-lanes, ancient ruins, and night life of Paris.
When I came to America a decade ago,
I was carrying a hangover of things past.

There comes a time in the life of all men and women,
When their relationship with all key facets of life undergoes a subtle change.
It may be a realization of what they mean to each other,
Or the realization of how they are influenced by the society and country they inhabit.

Maine first opened its heart to me when I visited Monhegan.
The Atlantic Island with its clear blue waters and rocky beaches,
The wooden cottages and towering lighthouse built for ancient mariners,
The glorious sunsets in the distance and artists galore capturing its essence.

The memories that lay dormant were fired up once again this summer,
As I finally came to fall in love with America and its rugged natural beauty.

Acadia's dawns over countless islands and cosmos-studded skies by deep night,

The green water and aged lighthouses,

The welcoming people,

The schooners drifting off by the piers on Bar Harbor,

The boat rides over the lake and the kids jumping off shallow cliffs;

America had it all and that was enough to set the heart throb.

This was a place to live a fruitful life,

No lesser than what any migrant leaves behind.

Mater Mine

There is a subtle switch between deep sleep and supramental awareness.
It is in that zone of total alertness and attunement to higher powers,
Do magical experiences happen;
And in that dimmed yet intensely penetrating backdrop,
Does Gurudev bring the resplendent mother to the beseeching seeker.

She is very beautiful and you can feel the kindest love she has for you.
You know everything will be alright, she doesn't have to say it.
Happiness, sorrow, anxiety, fear, angst,
All melt away and become petty sensations,
As she inspires you to connect with her,
Transcendentally in a superior way.

You just want to be with her, concentrate on her, and connect with her.
There is no time, no universe, no physics—just a glimpse of eternity.
This is a silence that goes on forever;
You lose your physical voice and the need to speak or communicate;
You stop thinking and your mind goes vacant.
An empty vessel for the mater to fill
In whatever way she likes.

In this conscious surrender,
You start exchanging mental thoughts;

And the message is loud and clear for you alone to hear,
The enchanting tolling of hallowed temple bells from a distance.

As you start descending from the heady heights of realization,
The active mind takes over again and begins to ask questions:
Why do we exist? Why were we created to be in constant suffering?
Why do the less fortunate undergo such unbearable agonies?
Why does she tolerate the utter cruelty of one for another?
What is her relation to Adinath? Why the dichotomy?
If everything is simply a state of mind,
Why do we have to bear the pain, whether ours or that of others?

The 'whys' go on with no answer,
An image remains in the mind.
Mater smiles and says, "enjoy the benediction first,"
In time, all questions will find satisfying answers.
When you are capable of bearing the truth,
The truth will be revealed to you, all in stages;
Akin to a progression of images towards a final conclusion.

The Married Monk

The married monk sits at his desk and invites the next seeker in.
A man and woman walk in, in distress –
Their son has gone astray.
The monk advises them on how to bring him back,
And assures them that all will be well.
They walk out with a measure of relief;
Just another day at the office,
As the doorbell rings again.

The next one in has lost his job,
And is barely making ends meet.
The monk hands him some money,
And gives him a number for finding a new vocation.
And so on and so forth, solving problems at the root;
The doors open and bring new supplicants,
And he continues doing his charitable work.

He heads home after a long day and night on the merciful chair;
Reaches home well past the dinner hour.
His wife feeds him dinner,
And asks why he needed a married life with her,
"If he needs nobody by his side".

He knows she is sad and that bothers him.
He strives to explain:
"I wanted you to share with me, an attachment-free life;
Devoted in service of suffering mankind".
And she ruminates on the answer,
Then lets go of her buffeting doubts
And understands after so many years
That she is in an existence,
Dedicated to the highest purpose man can have.

Even a man of God needs some time to himself;
And it's a Sunday—a time of rest and contemplation.
He strolls by nature's side,
And finds a nice black rock to meditate on.
He sits in lotus position and opens his third eye;
The essence of creation floats by in his mind's eye.
He dissolves in this light and is lost to the manifest Cosmos.
He stays thus for a blink of an eternal eye,
Which is the time taken for the sun to set.

Beyond the horizon,
The bite of an insect brings him out of his reverie.
He smiles at the feast that he provided to another of creation's creatures;
Giving till the end is his sacred purpose.
He heads home and goes to bed,
Preparing for another day in the cycle of life.

The Great Gurudev

He walks in through the door,
And my heart beats a special beat—a beat just for him;
A beat that does not resonate for anybody else.
This is a unique connection;
I was born to be his disciple and he my master.

He looks wonderful in blue, my favourite colour.
I ask him for a picture and he acquiesces;
This is a special moment and we both know that.
Will it come again? I don't know!
But one should be optimistic when faced with the vagaries of life.

And then he speaks in his unique voice,
Exuding power, eternal finality, and compassionate sweetness,
All at the same time.
And in that again I realize how fortunate I was,
To have his hand on my head all these years.
And in that understanding, I also admire
How he graced so many lives
While keeping the lowest of profiles.

I let the mind float, becoming a spectator,
As I listen to the conversation unfold.
He observes, assimilates, imbibes, and reflects and the insights flow.

I revel in the wisdom that is cast forth,
And internalize his approach to existence.
A learning applicable to all facets of consciousness and all walks of life –
The glimpse of mater in a divine dream
Had raised a lot of questions and I take the chance.
He says that Adinath decides where you land,
The mater Adi Maya helps you make the most of the landing.
The ultimate God created them both,
And both are incomplete without each other.
As we are incomplete without our counterparts
In all our planes of being—physical, astral, and mental.

The window of opportunity is closing,
The wheel of time decides how long an event can last.
And he is tiring, it's time to go.
I ask him about the blue pearl, the white pearl,
Or whatever coloured pearl one sees
And its relation to the flame.
He confirms that another dream is right.

The spinning pearl is not to be underestimated;
It created the universe and all that came from it.
The purpose of the flame is a conversation,
And an experience to be had in times to come.
The happiness of our meeting lingers on, even on distant shores.
Jai Guru Maharaj, Jai Gurudev!

The Curtain of Non-dualism

I ran into a wall, like I would into a curtain
With all colours including that of blood, heavy with blood.
I asked the wall for a solution, till I lost my voice
But got nothing in return.

With a very heavy head,
And feeling so feverishly tired all of a sudden,
I asked why the wall invoked
As much fear and dread as definitive calm.
The non-dualism voice answered as it sometimes does:
"You have to take the good with the bad,
You can't distil only the beauty out."

The wall spoke on further:
"Keep faith in love, that's where the shine comes from.
Since non-dualism is both misery and sorrow as well as eternal happiness,
You need to have the strength to bear a look back,
And look forward at the plethora of sentient agony".

That made sense!
This was the reality behind
What we all imagine as the ultimate enlightenment.
Whether called Brahman or 'no-mindedness' in the East,
The ultimate calmness is abiding with the varied hues we call 'existence'.

So as of today, with no answer in sight,

The curtain behind which hides the ultimate

Does offer an answer:

"It's a passing phase in the long journey called evolution.

Once you get used to it,

You will get a glance of me and the meaning of eternity."

My Mantra

I tried hard, persevered very hard but gave up in the end.

He said, "the world is just a dream"—but I disagree;

I love the various actors who populate this Earth,

And the Cosmos beyond reach quite unconditionally;

And grateful for them being there for me—making every moment worthy.

There might well and truly be a creation

Beyond what the mind's eye now sees;

But it should be possible to live in both of these quite simultaneously.

He said, "You are your own Guru, why do you need another one outside?"

And although this is possibly very true,

I would not discount the real Guru who raised me as a son;

Opening my mind to a love

That lies beyond the much touted 'romantic love';

Who suffered as I suffered, and cried as I cried;

Showering blessings of love with every word,

Enriching a life beyond what anyone could ever have imagined.

My mantra is: "We love, so we are."

I cannot fathom a dry world,

Where one searches for a mystical void.

He opened the door for a nirvanic connect

With energies that exist eternally,

And wait for you quietly to make the mark
To transcend into their realms,
Where it is always sunshine and early summer.
I will be eternally grateful for the love he held out for me;
The light in my existence,
A catalyst for my permanent foray into the state of *Turiya*.

We must all aspire to float out of our three bodies:
The physical, the astral, and eventually the mental;
Till we reach the point where we observe as spectators,
The workings of the body, the unconscious mind, and the spirit self.
Meditate with a loving heart,
And mount the wings of freedom and constant bliss;
That is my mantra, a constant way to be.

The Effulgent Adinath

Summertime is around the corner,
Sunshine in spring drags us to the beach.
Meditating by breaking dawn can be a rich experience;
But it is painful as we look back on the quickly passing years,
And reflect on all the suffering that surrounds us all the time.

It was a very long marriage but he passed away a few years ago.
She misses him horribly, a vacuum of loneliness that cannot be filled.
Sons and daughters and grandchildren can provide a measure of solace,
But practical limitations of myriad types can't make that happen.
Her shoulder hurts with each stretch for a chore;
Her knee hurts with each stair she climbs.
With nothing to look forward to really, what is the cure?

Children grew up fast, the elder son is on the cusp of leaving home;
The younger one has already started feeling the void he will leave behind.
With one gone and two to follow,
And occasional visits dwindling as the sons learn to forge their own lifestyle,
What will become of the parents who can keep in touch only through phone?

Does he eat well, does he have the right friends?
Does he cope with the academic workload, does he take good care of his health?

These swirling questions can bewilder by their intensity,
As you face your own problems
That develop one by one gradually with settling age.
You acutely become aware of all the tribulations of your parents
And wonder, with less and less to look forward to, what is the cure?

The promise of eternal life is not an empty promise.
Faith can make the breach bearable; spirituality can be a soothing balm.
It is real and not a flash of imagination, nor some fancy path of escapism.
The promise of the effulgent Adinath gracing your life
Is not just a form of surrealism.

He is there to be found within the mind's eye;
He is there in lotus position, exuding brilliant light, drawing us into him.
As we merge with him to the chants of "*Alakh Niranjan*",
He reminds us that this is the ultimate destination;
The *Turiya* of our eternal union is the cure you are all looking for;
The *Turiya* of this communion is what you should all look forward to.

The Greatest Romance of All

It's coming close to dawn, the picture flickers to a close;
It's about romantic love and the final consummation of a couple's trials
That sets me thinking—all relationships wane in the end;
Some before, some after, some in months and some in years to come.
Nothing lasts forever.

Children grow up and leave the nest;
We love them all our lives but as they mature into independency.
We come to learn that while the intensity of love
Continues in our heart and mind,
It is not quite the same as before.

And as I slip deeper into a meditative silence,
Accentuated by the stillness of 2 am,
The answer comes straight out of the blue.
The greatest romance of all is with God himself and his emissaries –
Whether it be Gurutattva or the golden-haired saints of the west.

The emissaries stand by us and guide us
Through a lifetime of pain and suffering.
Constantly within us, in a mantra, in a chant,
Through the warmth of a rosary bead,
Leading us into the beckoning beyond;
Beyond life and death, bursting into a consciousness of eternal life.

As you grow more attuned to their presence
And learn to tap into them at will,
The profound loneliness of existence fades away;
As you find their touch in the little things in life,
A sunset, a thunderstorm, a look on the face,
Tears streaming down a wet cheek.

This divine madness is the greatest bliss of all;
Their hand on your back, their light in your eyes,
Their scent in the air,
Their voice ringing through the inner ears,
This is the greatest romance of all –
One that never withers and never dies.

The Highest Height

Was creation born from light,
Or was it born from the sound of *Om*?
Did light produce *Om*?
Or did light emerge from the primordial sound?

I came with this question to the great Gurudev.
I sat in front of him for an hour,
And listened to him talk about his life experiences.
He mulled over a similar thought –
"As we attain absolute detachment, should we be detached from love too?"
He spoke for a while but concluded that we need love to live.

Becoming a pure spectator can happen in Advaita Vedanta.
So, I turned to the mind to unravel this truth for myself.
Consciousness turned to the God of non-dualism and said,
"We love, so we are."
Ending the academic debate inside and leaving no scope for confusion.

That also ended the dryness of knowledge-seeking,
And looking for love in all associations.
Detachment paves the way for all-abiding love,
Leading to love above detachment and not above love.

One can conclude that the super-consciousness of *Turiya* came first –
This always existed, rooted in sentient love;
Then came the light, the sound, and Maya
That created the manifest and unmanifest universe and the distinct soul.

The Blue Pearl

As you close your eyes and travel,
You will eventually encounter the ancient seer
Sitting in lotus position with gaze turned within
And meditating on the blue pearl that lies at the center of the human brain.

And in that meditative silence,
He casts forth a light from the pearl;
A divine light, an inviting light, an absorbing light
That welcomes souls to connect with him and his broadcasting pearl.

And when he connects with you, he inspires you, guides you, and motivates you
Into new endeavours, heightened thought, and headier emotional depths,
Providing a means to alternatively exist, beyond the boredom of complete detachment,
Emerging into pure consciousness as you find a reason for existing as a distinct being.

And while the seer is the one who brings out the hidden latent in us,
Let us not forget the mother who is present beyond him—who created him.
As a gift for creation's sentient souls to rejoice in, a conduit to see her ways,

She occasionally gives us glimpses of herself in various forms –
Discerned by the obsidian cobras and golden glow on the faces of those
she manifests on.

God Is a State of Mind

Time passes by so fast, a billion years doesn't seem like an eternity.

You look at your not-so-young face in the mirror,

And reflect on where all those moments went.

Reflecting on mortality, one is inevitably drawn to the ultimate question:

What is the nature of God and how do you get to him/her?

From a crushing separation from everything precious, how do you find a solace?

From loneliness, from pain, from the feeling of loss to the actual loss,

Where is he/she and how do you find him/her, ending the misery of a solitary existence?

God must be a state of mind is what the sentient mind replies.

God is a state of mind for the farmer who waits with bated breath for timely rains,

As he sows the first seeds that become his crops –

Hoping against all hopes that they do not fail and take his life with them.

God is a state of mind for the anxious lover

Who spends sleepless nights and aimless days hoping for her grace.

But when that grace does materialize,

It reveals its temporal nature, losing intensity in a year or two that they live together.

God is a state of mind for the new mother,

Her very breath stuck in every cry of her little child.

She loses her hunger, finding solace in every drop of milk that her baby takes.

She is one with her child and all motherhood.

This is a state of mind that lasts a lifetime but brings with it a never-ending anxiety.

There must be a higher feeling, a higher truth, a higher *raison d'être.*

While all these are God-like unifications, they don't last long.

And once past these, the seeker turns back to a more permanent answer;

And sometimes, it does materialize—the answer that is:

He drifts through a library, all the Swamis on book covers smile in benediction.

And in a corner is the energy source, source for all that drives creation.

He enters it briefly and dissolves into the oneness of God, one with everything.

Then down, as he exits, all life's problems start crowding into his mind;

But that state of mind is the final state of mind to strive for,

And there in is the reply, the final answer, the *coup de foudre* worth striving for.

Dissolution

The plane is in vertical ascent,
And so is the soul;
Reaching cruising altitude,
The soul bursts free in the rarefied air.

He slips into light sleep, more a trance than slumber;
The vibrations generated by the turbulence stir his heart.
The pounding begins, and his gut goes through a wrenching turmoil;
Energy is at play and one becomes a spectator in the unravelling scenes.

He slips deeper into the spell;
He tries desperately to quell the pounding breast,
All to no avail—the energy will listen to no one.
The message is clear—"Your time is here, and I will decide what happens now."
There is terror in his mind, of his responsibilities towards his children and their mother. He cannot be in a trance for days on end when there is work to be done;
The energy is compelling and heeds no one's pleading desperation.

This cannot be his time to merge!
The soul is on the verge of an explosion into the vast unknown.
Fear intensifies—what if there is no coming back from beyond the veil?
This is a moment of exaltation that is cherished forever!
But it cannot be his time.

He screams silently—"Stop", "Please let me go!"

And reinforces his will to stay in his mortal coil;

Somehow the energy listens—or not really.

This was just a taste of eternity.

There will be a next time, but it will all be smoothly done then;

The merged consciousness and the solitary soul will coexist at some future time.

On the Brink

It takes an eternity, to be on the brink of eternity.
After all that suffering, the promise of being finally free.
But that release into constant bliss can be an illusion,
Bringing more problems than can be solved.
Better to be very patient.

One has to be very patient because
The experience permanently alters consciousness.
You don't want to return as a raving lunatic with a body in tow,
Unable to cope with the enormously potent power of divinity.

And even if you do cope after the merging,
Assuming that you can come back,
You will be totally cleaved from daily living.
There will be no drive left to wage the daily battles of life,
Or strive every moment for the dependants in your life.

Dependants are called just that because they cannot do without you;
The guilt will be enormous if you can't do right by them.
You must learn to be detached and attached all at the same time,
And that is why diving from the brink is better done in short phases.

One day with luck, the golden balance can be achieved.
A consistent and constant state of *Turiya*,
Cognizant of life's pressures and pulls—achieving permanency,
When nothing is left behind.

A Compassionate Soul

She wakes up in the morning at the crack of dawn;
It's a bit cold in the mountains even at the peak of summer.
A new day, a continuing mission that she committed herself to, a long time ago.
She wonders at the thoughts that flow by, like a stranger watching herself.
For a moment, she has lost the feeling of 'I', the solitary being.
She has a name, an identity, and memories from which she is completely detached.

She has a mission and there is no time to reflect on such transcendental states of mind.
By day, she passes on the knowledge and wisdom she has learned,
Creating an infectious thirst for comprehension and insight in her wards;
Those bequeath to her for a variety of reasons covering the coloured spectrum of light.

She is more than a teacher of letters and words, of chapters and verse;
She is a mother, a confidante, and at times a constant guide to the young minds
Who love her as much as she loves them, as she consoles them by night,
Clearing the tear from each weeping eye, silently but surely
Making sure that the tender psyches are ready to face the world outside.

In that commitment of the perfectly compassionate soul,
In crossing the chasm from teacher to bearer of the light,
There is a cross to bear and a price to pay.
She has no time and space to indulge her personal likes and dislikes.
Today, she wears on her worried brow,
The coming of age pains of someone abandoned;
Working out how to solve the problems that are more imaginary than real.

She has the touch of the mother, the energy that created us all;
And the mother motivates her along, giving her a higher reason and purpose.
And that makes her special, her mission stands her apart;
She has gone far beyond, working for a living or enjoying a professional life.
She is a vital cog in the wheel of creation that spins forever on.

A Thousand Petals Blooming

First the light begins to settle, a golden yellow hue.
Low key but full of energy and vibrance,
A few souls sit around the small stone parapet.
Someone comes in and says a few words in praise of God;
Of one specific religion but the message is that of peace and harmony.
Not dualism or distinction, but the fact that all roads lead to the same place.

For the listeners of the divine message,
This is a moment of infinite empowerment;
A right to live and believe in a transcendental state,
To practice spirituality in a way that is correct and path-setting in all ways.

It is all for the better if the blessing is smooth.
It settles, it changes, it leaves, and yet changing perception forever.
You find futility in negativity and boundless energy of positivity,
All abiding love and compassion for all emanations of creativity.

You learn to trust, to have faith;
All that seems bad will come good;
All that seems insurmountable will dissipate gradually.
You come to detach yourself from any aspect of consciousness
That causes unbearable pain.

You will let go and the flying will begin,
Light as a feather, floating on the divine breeze that carries you on.

An Alternate Life

The saffron and white coloured robes exert an exquisite pull.
To don them, free of worldly possessions, free of monetary commitments,
To devote your life to being a man of God,
All thoughts absorbed in devotion to the Almighty Lord,
Leading a procession with clanging cymbals,
Singing hymns that take you to headier heights.

You wander the lands, collecting alms from some open doors;
Sometimes spoilt, sometimes dry,
Just enough to assuage the occasional hunger;
Yet so delicious as, it befits an alternate life;
An affirmation of values that bind the soul to the harsh choices they made.

Sitting on a mat under the shady trees, in the cool breeze,
Absorbed in silence, as fellowmen hold discourses on ancient texts,
All in praise of the lord—as the chanting begins once again,
You contemplate the myriad insects that wander over your legs,
Relishing a savoury bite.

Even a life dedicated to the divine can bring an attendant reputation.
The poor, the needy, and those in the throes of suffering,
Flock to you as you strive to bring them relief.
In serving these people, you discover a higher purpose,
As you contemplate why so much grief was ever created in the first place.

If you are chosen, this question is answered and all questing ceases.

Whether misery brings higher devotion,

And whether it is the beginning and end of all craving.

One will never know, for those who know will never tell.

An alternate life is a huge challenge that draws in only those who feel the urge:

Beyond poverty, beyond disease, beyond the whitening hair and failing health,

A ship cast on rough seas, completely at the mercy of the swirling winds.

Basking Ridge

It's another cold February morning in Basking Ridge;
The snow storms have plied their misery aplenty this year.
For the children it's a novelty, as they spend days cloistered at home or
school.
Life's a lot more painful for the parents who venture far and wide for
work;
And further more for those who can't afford
The luxury of a shelter and warm clothes.

As the streets are cleared by shovel and truck, by a hint of sunshine and
some rain,
I ponder over my new home, our town—a new America, a new society;
Wondering what Emily would have made of this, if she availed her choice –
Deciding to be born with a little help, in this suburban town many miles
from New York.

Every school of thought from east to west, has a different take on the
afterlife;
Some say she would be born to fulfil her latent wishes and desires,
Some say she would be given a life that aligns with her deeds of past lives.
And some simply say,
The masters of afterlife gave her a chance to grow and evolve
In a new setting, a new culture, and a new time with advancements of
many kinds.

What would her existence be in the new milieu?

Better healthcare for one, none of the business of dying in childbirth;

The ultimate in unnecessary suffering, dying as a bundle of delight comes to life;

And better education, a choice of professions for those inclined to a working life.

Better civil liberties for sure, and more respect for women's rights;

She would be happy I guess, being spoilt for choice.

But every blessing comes with a hidden downside;

The level of integration and sheer warmth of a community she would find declined.

And in that is the ultimate lesson –

Never compare, never look forward, nor look back;

The moment you live in is the best moment that you can have.

To adapt and forget would be the best way to move on.

And so, we hope that if she were to grace our town,

It would not be as the Emily of the past,

But as a Sarah or Jane of the current or future!

Black Belts

They were just babies, cute and soft and very cuddly!
Now I watch in awe, as they break cinder blocks in a stroke!
It has been four years from the day they dropped their first punch;
I never realized that one day I would be a proud father,
Watching them don their black belts.

They struggled through their essays, searching deep inside for meaning.
But it all came out well, in their amateur ways.
They learned how to express their feelings,
They endured the pain that comes with practicing and perfecting form;
And cried occasionally through the physical exercise
That seemed at times beyond their years.

It is easy to be sceptical but I was converted on the testing day.
The masters put the students through their paces,
And it all came together making perfect sense;
The fasting, the midnight training,
The bonds that they forged with student and instructor alike,
The creation of a family, away from a family;
The Dojang as a home away from home.

Whatever the discipline, whatever the walk of life,
The master-disciple tradition
Is one of passing on the message of love in excellence.

Love for all, a non-judgemental love,
A love that does not feel separation when apart,
A love that strives for a permanent unification,
That is the destination of Advaita too!
All is one, all are one, and the almighty permeates all.
The Guru in the Nath order and the Master in Tae Kwon Do
Both have a singular purpose
Of preserving the flame of knowledge and values—and beyond that, wisdom
As each new generation goes through the rite of passage.

I am glad and content, it is a big achievement;
All those unique experiences they have gained.
They are little men now, bigger than their size might indicate,
Now cast in the mould of what their masters construed.

Center of the Universe

Another snow-flaked festive eve, first Christmas, now 2013's end-to-be;
Too cold to venture into Times Square, too cold to see the ball drop.
And as the commentator said, "The city is the center of the universe tonight!"
It set me thinking about why we didn't quite empathize with his P.O.V.

One decides one's own center, you know!
It could just as well be by a howling street dog in Mumbai as you try to sleep,
Or a night by the TV in Pune, huddling around with friends and family.
A coffee in a Starbucks could do just as well,
If you felt right with the moment that was being revealed.

That brings us to the old immigrant workers' tale –
Circumstances and fate drive him out of his home to find another nest,
And the nest never quite replaces the one he left behind.
And while his kin is bettered by the fostering nation he finds,
He never quite overcomes or forgets the little cultural icons left behind:
The favourite snacking joint, the beauty down the street, or an institutional canteen,
The concern in a mother's call for supper or a sisterly scolding laced with advice.

The ultimate dream remains a constant needle in his thoughts,
The craving to find his center again.
The security that lies over and above all the gains and losses in life,
A promise for a kind of happiness that incessantly torments by its absence.

Future Promise

[Open with an A7, Em, D, and E arpeggio]

It was a life cut prematurely short, [A7]
She could have done so much more! [Em]
Sometimes, the future can bring us home; [D]
Trust God to save us from a fall. [E]

[Small lead in scale]

I heard the sweetest boy talk,
Not a bad way to come out.
We will wait and we will watch,
We do connect somewhere we know not.

[4 chord arpeggio]

Memories linger on, as she does on some unknown platform;
There is always a lesson to be learned and I have learned mine.
Be very attentive to the present,
And never hurt anyone—in that are the seeds of future self-destruction.

[4 chord arpeggio]

Reunification

Another euphoric reunion comes to an end,
And we fly off to where we came from.
More memories created, more hearts touched,
Many songs and dances performed.
The romantic, the philosopher, the king of one-liners,
The athlete, the intellectual, the business professional,
All come together with no distinction;
All joined together in one cosmic revolution,
Fuelled by alcohol and laced with love and devotion.

Partings are always painful,
Whether touched with tears or without.
But the truth is, we never part;
We are bound together in eternal bonds on some mystical plane.
Our love for each other, matured and cured by time,
Will survive the usual odds.

The multi-year brutal immersion was
As much about knowledge gained,
As it was about discovering each other,
And the associations that would last a lifetime.
I used to think that every life is a book;
But I saw a voyage and realized that
Each life is closer to a journey, than a chapter or verse.

The teenage years, the early adulthood, the travel through vocational years,
The wisdom gained, the cultural experiences gathered,
The joy, the pain, the grace, and the knocks of daily living,
They would all etch fine lines on the psyche
That make each individual different.

And as collegemates, I hope we continue to cherish our relationships;
God knows there are millions of reasons just waiting to waylay us humans.
It is a progression rather than an end,
As our friendships blossom over the years.
It is this friendship we savour
That can help solve all the problems we harbour,
Rather than falling prey self-consciously to
Gender, religion, and myriad considerations.

Reunification No. 2 – To Us

As we resume our daily regimes and tend to the exigencies of a working life,
It behoves us to contemplate what lies ahead and how to deal with it.
To start with, acknowledgement of how privileged we and our kids are,
To have a cohort group of such high standing and class.

My mind often reflects on the have-nots—the young children and men,
Without food, without sanitation, without medication, without homes,
Leave alone education.
While our mantra is a cool, "We don't need an education!"
The teeming masses cry in despair, "If only we could have an education!"

As we get older, our health will fail gradually;
Our children will fly the nest,
And we will have to deal with the vacuum they leave behind.
This circle will be our last resort,
Inspiring us to battle the obstacles and excel,
Rather than cope with our future lives.

I wonder why we were never so open,
And unreserved with each other at the start.
Why didn't we trust each other?
Was it societal pressures and general expectations?
I am glad that now rather than never, we are so warm with each other.

Having each other in the Promised Land is the greatest treasure of all.
We are a support system that will never get disillusioned with time.
We have each other, to hold on to when comes the time.
The best years are still to come rather than gone,
Is a point of view, a perception we have to reinforce with due diligence.

Reunification No. 3 – The Rose Queens

She didn't set out to break any hearts,
As she stepped into the campus for the first time.
She was always beautiful, to the point that she didn't realize.
The day was but a few hours old, when she got her first invite for tea.
'No' was a response most expected—she was too young to grapple with society.

As the months rolled on, she came to be as loved as she was hated;
Loved publicly, vociferously, unabashedly, and unequivocally,
And hated privately—"Who did she think she was!"
Either way, she didn't ask for the turmoil;
She just wanted a normal college life.

There is a price to be paid for anything good in life,
And her personality came to be summarized as a queen of roses.
Only she knew the extent of the thorns that pricked her,
The constant barrage, the lack of privacy, and the distortion of self-identity.

As time rolls inexorably on, the human mind learns to numb pain.
In time, she learned to ignore the adulation and the barbs,
The puerile romantics and the sometimes-envious sisters.
With a dulled sensitivity—existence became suddenly bearable.

All was not bad though, as the years passed;
There came a greater acceptance of her need to be left alone.
The attention waned and she even came to like someone;
Though she could not do anything, as it was not allowed.

Who said being a queen of hearts was a coveted position?
Far more attractive it is, to be a normal person.
Who said it was easy being a woman in those times and these?
Mostly being misunderstood is the fate of most women to this day.

Tête-à-Tête Avec Mon Fils

The lights are out, the sun is fading,

It is dark blue on the horizon with orange shots.

Not used to living in the dark, everyone is out walking around impatiently;

We sit by the sliding doors, watching the fireflies flicker intermittently.

It's a cool night; we synchronize our souls to pass time instead of becoming comatose

By a modern light source spewing song, dance, and convolutions.

Junior and I spoke sweet nothings

That will become cherished memories for tomorrow.

The elder one is nine and junior is six, so I started things off.

"Senior's entry into my life brought me unbounded happiness," I tell him.

"And junior's entry into my life brought about a turnaround in our well-beings."

And so junior asks me, "Dad, are you sad that I came three years late?"

So, I ask him why he didn't come down along with senior.

He says, "Ask God, only God will know why he kept me three years longer."

"But if I had a choice, I would have come the very next day!"

But our chats are not always a happy arithmetic.

He understands that we had three years more with his elder brother

And then he is sad, briefly not too deeply, though touchingly.
I missed so much with Mum and Dad.

It's hard accounting for such gains and losses
But he wraps up my evening by saying, "I love you".
I ask him, "How much?" and he says, "A million".
"Is that all?" I ask and he replies, "Much more than that!
Actually, the last number on planet Earth, more like!"

Thank You

As the man says,
When you move from 'have to' to 'get to',
Existence becomes a long list of 'Thank You's.
And two days off the grind become
More than an American holiday season.
And in that spirit of appreciating all within and without:
Thanking the unseen for providing the skills
To write these words that you read out aloud.

Where do you kick off the list?
What would life be without my two sons and extended ones?
Sure, one day they will leave the nest and we will miss them so much
But until then, appreciate the next ten years that lie ahead.

A big thank you to the elders who covered me in warm blankets
As the night grew dark and cold at times.
Much appreciation to my wife who with her unflinching love,
Broke down every callus that had formed in the heart
Over the first thirty years of my life.

And finally, though each day can seem like an ordeal at times,
Grateful I am for the company of men and women who stand together,
One in spirit and endeavor, braving the vagaries of commercial existence,
Together as one family, as one light that burns bright,
Making comfortable and cosy, what would otherwise be a desolate life.

The Caregiver

There are many definitions for greatness.
Some believe that greatness is in excellence –
In the arts or science or medicine or technology.
But there are those who are chosen by Adinath,
Due to their innate goodness and compassion for people.

He is and always has been an exemplary caregiver;
Whether it was his ailing mother or father,
Whether his children or the large flock of nephews and nieces.
He always stood by them through thick and thin,
Never expecting anything in return, even as a word.

A wise man once said—no one knows why good people attract much
suffering.
And while there is no answer, he never complained
As he provided a quality education for his nears and dears
Through his constant struggles with Asthma
While working his life in the factories, which were never good for his
health.

I will always remember our summer vacations at his place,
His unique googly as he knocked out my stumps in the old Rama temple;
His open door for a meal as I sickened of the ordinary canteen fare,
And the crutches he brought me when I first broke my leg.

He will soon be seventy-five but he leads by example,
To find peace and contentment in service of even a sliver to mankind.
He is a loving soul,
And that is all that Adinath ever expected of us –
That solitary hallmark of greatness
That manifests as the mangoes he brings
For the next generation he adores.

The Feet of Gurudev

It took a long time to fall in love
But I did eventually.
It is exhausting beyond words to conceptualize Advaita,
The rest is best left unsaid, I'm afraid.

The long drive back is easier than the long one forward;
It's an early night and I lie down after putting the kids to bed.
The energy is back and invites me to journey…
I decline; this intensity is enough for me.
I can't handle this transcendental complexity.
Giving up, I descend from where I was all day,
Into what is a more refreshing sleep.

Enlightenment does not stop the crying;
It only makes you more acutely aware of the misery that surrounds us
perennially.
The ecstasy and the pain of anguish have blended together into a
riveting mix;
You need to get comfortable to face a revival of memories.

For me, this is the happiness I seek;
And as we say our farewells to each other,
He says, "Your destination is at the feet of Gurudev,
Stop scribbling at this stage and leave your guitar in its case!"

I agree, this state of being doesn't need any further gratification,
Though it's always safe to include some practicality in your daily life.
Co-existence on multiple levels is the ideal way,
And knowing which facet to indulge at what stage is a wise choice.

The splitting headaches are now overwhelming and I need some solace.
I get home and call him—"Why don't I ever feel the touch of Gurudev?"
"You will, you will," he says.
Twilight falls, my favourite time of the day.
The chants of *Om* start ringing through the dark confines of the universe;
The saffron sounds fill my head and the pain disappears—I am rejuvenated.
Jai Guru Maharaj, Jai Gurudev!

The Heroes That We Forgot

Life can be very difficult if you are not a successful renunciant or working class;
Survival can be hand-to-mouth existence, from shelter to feeding your flock.
You need an education to rise above the teeming lots scrambling for jobs;
Somewhere in the race, we failed to sing a song for the heroes that we forgot.

We reserve a joke or two for them at alumni meets.
We believe the institution made us what we are,
Rather than those who manned the towers.
In our fine suits and flashy cars and even if we be as ordinary as we are,
We never quite recognize the efforts they took to make us who we are.

God knows they were far from perfect but they had our best at heart;
It was fashionable to rebel, so we did—against the subject and so against its exponent.
We had our own insecurities and failings, so we shot salvos wherever we could;
Never realized that they did what they did out of a passion to mould our pliable minds.

Sure, there is the odd rotten apple who peers below the desk,
Or achieves sadistic pleasure
In making us shed a bucketful of tears in fearful dread.

But over and above, are those who ply
With little appreciation and smaller salaries to speak of,
With the singular aim of providing us
The tools that we need to stand on our own feet.

We forgot them as we stepped out of the corridors;
Some died painful deaths and some just withered away.
We should have made an annual pilgrimage to touch their feet,
And remind them that their forbearance and patience was not in vain.
But we rarely did—rather,
We remember them through stories of how we subverted their best intent,
Scoffed at their tattered clothes and loneliness,
That set in as the sun set on the paths they once walked.

They helped us then, we can help them now;
A little recognition is in order for the heroes that we forgot.
Just an acknowledgement, a small thank you can warm the heart;
We still have a chance to turn back the clock.

The Times with Gurudev

He is scary, you know, and the things he controls can frighten you;
A glimpse into his thoughts can probably permanently paralyse you.
But as I wear my clothes and start the morning early with a spring in my step,
He sends me a silent message, "I love you son, so go forth and blossom!"
And with the hand of Adinath on your head, nothing can go wrong.

A winter morning is a double-edged sword;
Sometimes magical for the chill and freshness in the air, and for the silent sparrows,
Sometimes surreal for the ancient swirling memories it brings to the fore.
For me today, it reminds me of all my times with Gurudev.

The lessons of love, pain, and endurance,
The patient attention, a study in devotion,
A fulcrum in an otherwise meandering life, a call to action,
A constant reassurance in an otherwise constantly fluctuating world.

And so, with all the fond remembrances of my youth,
The times with Gurudev is a strength that will live forever.
And while separation can cast an unwieldy pall and sadden the heart,
Gurudev assures that the time and space of distances are a mere illusion.

You can sit in NYC and still be in the resplendent Himalayas.

You can be sitting alone and still be with me.

Our hearts are one and that's all that matters.

Reflect on the dichotomies that don't exist and you will find your answers.

The *Turiya* of Silence

The only real silence is in the stillness of the mind.
When thoughts either cease or flow through without casting ripples,
The need to communicate is either driven by a need and a desire,
Or by a higher purpose, in which case a perfect harmony is realized.

There are many first steps on the path to enlightenment.
Some start with controlling breath;
Some start with immersion and losing oneself in melodic sound;
Some start with renunciation, sacrifice, and strict penance;
But the practice of silence, both verbal and telepathic, is something special.

The start of verbal silence is also the start of the practice of tolerance.
Holding your consul, holding back convincing for self-gain,
Holding back emotional expression –
You learn to let go, fall back in rhythm with the higher self, inside and above;
And as you move from apprentice to adept, the subliminal voices begin to be heard.

What is the source of the subliminal messages that start to permeate the mind?
It is the collective consciousness of the higher realms that exist beyond imagination.

The deepest sub-conscious fears and impulses are pacified, then satisfied;
And some years later, you find that even these flow by as the "I" gradually disappears.

In that perfect mental and spiritual vacuum, the highest sound begins to reverberate.
The saffron *Om*, the blue *Om*, the luminescent *Om*, in sound and soundlessness,
Fill the void with an ultimate reality that descends smoothly.
In *Om* is the silence we crave and seek all our existence.
Not a silence without a sound
But the silence of all that distracts and torments all states of mind;
In that *Turiya*, we are not passive;
We are merely spectators of the highest will,
As we do and don't on the path called evolution.

The White Flame

It's summer again—blue skies, the sun shines bright;
The fragrance of cut grass threads through the air.
Young children frolic in perfectly cut lawns and vacant streets,
And new life takes form as nature's silent miracles seep in.

The white flame with a bluish tinge embraces the blue pearl,
And in the realization of something very precious,
The mind gravitates again to listen
To the thoughts and cries of those less fortunate,
As they all merge into one expression of sentiment.

The flame is a flame of wisdom and the awareness of universal pain
Bestowed on the capable, by the father and mother of the Nath order.
The merging of Adinath and Adi Shakti, the essence of their spirits,
Bringing a heightened awareness of unified sentient feelings.

The heart beats faster, as an indescribable anxiety grips the being.
Intellect and emotions from uncountable souls surge through the mind.
There is no justice for all; to avoid your suffering, you need to go above it.
Aspire for the flame, aspire for detachment, and devotion will set you free.

Once free, you will fly above all that holds you down.
Some anguish might remain but that will remain on the ground.
As you soar, spreading your wings,

Higher and higher, from plane to plane,
Driven by the flame into a blue-sky world distinct from yours,
It's summer again—voices of angels and cherubs ring through the ears;
It's just a different realm, a different state of mind.

The Inevitable

The haves and have-nots are lining up for a massive collision again.
This time, it is the very fate of feeding a hungry mouth at stake.
But in that sense, it is no different from previous revolutions –
The asymmetrical distribution of wealth in extremis is the cause again.

The brilliant, the rich, and the powerful are in an unwitting or maybe witting nexus;
He who replaces the most humans wins the game –
Of prestige, intellect, peer approval, and money,
Forgetting that the only real game in town is the common good of mankind;
Some return their spoils as charities for food and water,
Giving through one hand to compensate taking away through many others.

Shiny new toys, both touchable and untouchable are for us, not for them.
This time, there might be no other means to provide livelihoods.
New leaders will emerge and wide-scale upheavals might be the norm,
As humankind tries hard to protect itself from its own.

Maybe finer sense will prevail earlier than later,
And we can be spared another failed attempt at socialism and more.
Maybe governments will step in with bans and controls
Before it is too late and we all gravitate towards the inevitable –
A generation of gloom, doom, and temporary resurrections.

We must control, do what is good for the evolution of society;
From illiteracy to enlightenment, from living in filthy hovels to sanitary sublets.
This is the challenge before us—not trying to throw ourselves out
But using our brains to find a way to improve the masses.

A Twenty-Year View

As I climb down the stairs, I say her name again and again
Till it sounds foreign, the person behind it someone new.
It's a clean slate in which I begin to paint fresh colors;
And with that objectivity established, I see her in new light.

It's been twenty years together!
I could spend an eternity with her, so comfortable has the journey been.
Mostly up than down is the dominant theme;
I start to count the blessings that lay scattered in between.

She is so committed to the family
Almost to a fault, I asked her once if she could be anybody else.
She said she chose us and these are no light words;
You have to just imagine a bit of her to see how true that is.

We look at our two lovely boys who bind us together.
Beyond the occasional bickering and petty fights,
They strengthen our love as we head into the twilight years,
Laying to rest the first one who never saw the light.

And I love her more with each growing day.
Once the initial flush wears off, what shines through is
Her every moment of immersion in our family and our welfare.
If that isn't dedication and purity of mind and soul, I wonder what is!

PART II – MIDDLE YEARS IN INDIA

That Which You Always Have

Whether you care about rebirth or not, the afterlife or this one now,
Sit back, relax, stop your mind, stop your thoughts; let events flow.
Suspend everything, imagine illumination; it can just happen, you know.
Looking back at your youth, tell yourself, "Twice the same is never done."
Look upon the happiness of others and participate, be happy for them.
Hope for eternal bliss, not just painful realizations, as you grow old.

Heaven across the wall, I am somebody you are not.
Angry and insecure, anxious chips of golden blocks.
Nothing bequeath, nothing achieved, days pan into dawns and dreams.
Renounce, turn off the light, there is no escape of a lasting sort.

Hurting me, hurting you, we are enmeshed like there is no two;
Accept and survive, drift like a Windsor swan on a tranquil Thames.
Cast away the bitter moments of disappointment that seem unending;
Realize their nature—artificial, immaterial, and altogether external.
Happiness is making the most of sunshine and gloomy thunderstorms;
Beyond ego and 'I', happiness is seeing good in wickedness all around.

That which you always have, the celebration of consciousness and life,
Of love and optimism, of richness of deed and thought, a vibrant mind;
Beyond the nagging voice and caustic tongue, constantly finding fault,
That which you always have, a happiness nobody can take away from you.

The Path to *Turiya*

The path to *Turiya* is littered with sufferings of many kinds;
Some self-inflicted, some inherited, and some simply pointless.
Beyond the success and glamor we chase in the name of existence,
Turiya is the final reward that lies at the end of all our struggles.

Detachment will get you there;
Detachment from happiness, sadness, even love and joy.
You find your core, the flaming ball that lies inside;
It was cast in the mould of the supreme soul, which has no shape or form.

And it is a paradox actually;
For once you get into *Turiya*, the crying will begin once more.
You will cry at the inhumanity of mankind, the sheer neglect of the orphans;
You will cry for hours at the misery that dogs us as we get old and cold;
At the profound sadness of leading a dreary life;
Your denied dreams and aspirations, committed to being ordinary.

But the tears are the tears of *Turiya*.
They flow of their own accord, without wetting the core.
In *Turiya*, there is no need to strum a guitar or scribble some pretty prose;
You will feel better as you float above everything that tries to hold you close.

In *Turiya* is the answer to why we were cast out of heaven,
To go through the unending cycles of life and birth.
I hope I get there one day and I hope the same for you.
For, in *Turiya* is the peace that passes understanding,
And the love that passes possessing.
He has the answer but he will never tell you.
For, this is the answer above all, that really matters to me and you.

Advaita Vedanta

It's a long drive through the mountains covered with low-hanging mist.
The trees glisten green with condensation,
And streams gush pristinely through ancient cliffs.
This is the land of the mystics.
"Open and reach out through the ethereal eye," they insist.
And as I do, I realize—like the peace that passes understanding,
There is love that passes possessing.

And as I slip into a trance,
I realize that the metaphysical connect of pure pulsing energy
Is the love that we seek but never quite achieve.
It holds, it absorbs, and the distance of miles and confines of time desist.
The past never was and the future never will be.
The energy that is matter and light at the same time
Casts a pall on all clamouring of physical intimacy.

As the trance gets deeper and my destination beckons,
The ocean of Advaita asserts itself:
"There is no 'I' and no 'We', no thought, no emotion—only a limitless bliss."
Beyond the throbbing fronds, this is the joy that holds your heart and expands it gradually.
The mind dissolves; the heart soars and soars into the light
And becomes one with all that exist.

All we little elements of creation float in this singular sea –

The sea is in us and us in the sea.

The truth is tantalizingly close but a veil beyond reach.

The ultimate question is still unanswered, after which all craving will cease:

If all is one, why were we cast out of the light to be in constant unease?

L'Etude in Search of an Objective

He craves to remain perennially in *Turiya*,
Beholding mother in her fearful form, surrounded by swirling hymns.
Bells toll as blue and white luminous clouds slip in and between;
The immersion is complete and there is nothing remaining.

Much as he loves all and perceives acutely the facets of human suffering,
The bonds of earth and beyond exasperate endlessly;
The need to make ends meet, the incessant call to work.
To exist by a clock, in someone else's hand to wind;
What does it mean to be alive, when winter is at its height?

The love of God and the love of man are not necessarily distinct themes.
There is a time and place for every association, which is when the bloom
is realized.
Any attraction is ultimately short-lived and comes to a sudden end.
What is the purpose of *L'Etude* is that which he constantly questions.

Maybe, just maybe, in the undeniable energy connection that
revitalizes them
Is the answer that he seeks: *L 'Etude's* mission probably to pass on insights
of the line.
But the spiritual process being as democratic if not more than the
worldly one;

It must be by choice—while the flame and sphere of wisdom choose the beholder,
The beholder must also choose to accept the benediction,
Which can be a blessing or a bane, depending on the point of perception.

L'Etude is a Study in Patience

Love is felt; expression is fulfilling a want for something.
Turiya is floating under the blue skies, in cool waters,
Basking in white light and a faint breeze.
I see a temple and it is devotion and the devotee;
No one knows why we were cast out of the light to be in constant unease.

Death is not the end of life—consciousness lives forever on.
Pain is what we fear, the pain that we will fail to endure.
The transition hurts but we move from one life to another.
No one knows when and why we move from one to the other.

He asked for peace and freedom from suffering for all of creation.
He was the youngest one in the line.
Sometimes, I realize now what he meant…
When I see them in pointless torment,
I wish for them the calmness of enlightenment and the end of all that tension.

If you search long enough and are patient long enough,
The essence of the Guru will give its wise touch;
All answers will be illuminated and the intense restlessness will cease;
You will become one with all situations and its participants.

Since my sons' birth,
I have lost my feeling of loneliness in their silent pampering.
They pamper me and not me, them.
They care about me and will be there with me
On the journey that forward remains.

No verse is ever complete without dedication to Adinath.
With every breath you breathe, visualize the saffron *Om* that flows in and out.
All that you do will be fine,
And all that you don't will be even better.

Jai Guru Maharaj!
Jai Gurudev!

L'Etude Sur Mes Enfants

It's a somnolent Sunday morning, with a nice breakfast settling in late;
I drift into *Turiya*, generally wondering where life goes next.
I look at my white hair and realize that it is not that which makes me feel aged;
It is the speed at which *mes enfants* are growing up that suddenly makes me feel old.

One is seven and the other is four, seems only a while ago
That I brought them home from the hospital in their first clothes.
As I slip deeper into my reverie,
I peep into the future, lacing foresight with hindsight,
Finding that there is some fear that wakes me up with a thudding breast.

They have flown the nest, settled in lands far and wide, with their own broods.
And in that future, facing my own mortality and their absent presence,
I realize how difficult it will be to live without them.
They are happy and grown but there is an inevitable vacuum they leave behind.

And then as I come out with a racing pulse,
His sweet gargling laughter and lisping voice fill my heart with joy.
While the future will inevitably pose a challenge for man to resolve,
For the moment, *mes enfants* fill my life with all the love I could ever want.

And in the end, the only epitaph worth carrying is the one that says,
"Abundant love graced his life and so he went out with a smile!"

Resurrection

There is a certain *'je ne sais quoi'* in the atmosphere of ancient towns…
A connect with the long-gone spirits that spur you on.
From the inspirational touch of the blue spheres that spin forever on,
There comes a resurrection that erases memories and spreads a soothing balm.

Paris is rain-swept, and so is London town.
Poignant remembrances embrace the raindrops
That fall to the ground and leave the frown.
All the missed turns that occasionally haunt are finally resolved
And a little imagination converts what could have been anguish into an art form.

Night falls and I put the boys to bed.
In their innocent love and absolute cuteness, what could I ever want?
The notion of beauty undergoes a subtle transformation as the years roll on.
What could have been doesn't seem to prick anymore
And the magic of the "now" that permeates all future holds you on.

It doesn't always take nails to make a cross.
So, while the heart felt and no sounds could ever come out,
With a gentle support in the way you want comes a silent undramatic turnaround;

In time, you realize that save for eternal bliss, no happiness is ever permanent
And suffering is only a self-inflicted state of mind.

So, while there can linger a little regret, it helps to strive into action more.
For, in perfect contentment is the end of evolution of the human form.

Beautiful Miss M

The girls in A are better than the boys in E.
They pour over grades all night and pin up pie charts for all to see.
You'll get a frown if you ask what's the fuss about.
Yes, beautiful Miss M, we grin (only if you know the game you are playing).

They are breeding winners in school.
If you don't fit, you are a blundering fool!

Our great leaders started this adventure off.
We gotta do justice to their pictures on the wall.
Don't smoke in the Johns when bells go ringing at dusk
And show some respect to the girls as they walk past in their pretty gowns.

They are breeding winners in school.
If you don't fit, you are a blundering fool!

Long lines on winter mornings resisting the force-feeding of you.
Most went around in green, while some wore only blue.
Cocking a snook and smug that we are too clever to confuse,
Attempting to snuggle up at moments opportune and only getting further confused.

They are breeding winners in school.
If you don't fit, you are a blundering fool!

You don't know what it's like to be mad;
You don't know what it's like to sit in an unfeeling daze.
You are on a visit to another stinking sanatorium.
You settle for cutting grass
And leave the letters to somebody new (somebody smarter than you).

They are breeding winners in school.
If you don't fit, you are a blundering fool!

Screening you, they say, "sing a song" but you pointedly refuse.
"What do you think of beautiful Miss M?" and you play the blundering fool.
You play the blundering fool and say you never think of her that way.
But all the lads think of her no other way and know she's gonna be gone soon.
She's getting married, you know?
She's got a guy somewhere that nobody knows.

They are breeding winners in school.
If you don't fit, you are a blundering fool!

In From the Cold

Went in search of the mother divine,
Found instead the fostering mind:

> There is no paradise in this land
> That helps you get inside your human side.
> Went in search of eternal life,
> Found in it a kind of suicide.

Went abroad deciding to think on my own,
He set off the wheels and spun me across the Cosmos.
"That was it!" I thought, when I came out of the cradle,
The room began to resonate to the whirring of spindles:

> "It's all coming to an end," I heard,
> "Courage, son, courage! You shouldn't so easily buckle."

He's got a chant that he repeats to himself:
"I am the chosen one, I must not fail!"
"I am the chosen one, I must not fail!"
What are you gonna do when you fall from heaven?

> His piety is certainly a laugh;
> He couldn't hold on to dignity to save his life.

His rituals are an intricate fuddle.
Strips down to his vest and sits on a saddle;
Rings a bell and sings like a drunk;
Starts clapping when he reaches the final sequence:

> Did you find your answers or are you doping yourself?
> Did you get anywhere beyond tiring yourself?

In mental exhilaration might be a strange satisfaction.
The middling of reality and fictitious horizons;
The jumping up and down on the smallest of instance;
There might be a pleasure in not being an adult:

> Attempt to stir that dormant tide,
> Open up to sensitivity and greater insights.
> The child within is dead and the story is lost;
> Musing in verse got me out of the frost.

The blue circle and the white cloud
I fall asleep watching them flit across:

> Did he have to make the house rumble?
> Did he have to give me a fright?
> A hushed whisper in my ear would have been nice!
> I can see him chuckling, "That served him right!"

Oblivion

But for life, it was a good dinner otherwise;
Oblivion when you switch off the lights kissing the wife goodnight:

In search of the perfect verse,
In search beyond the makers of the universe,
In quest of better and best,
We ran through all the blood in our works.

Children left the nest, never call, always busy;
Nobody needs me, remembers me, loves me;
Oblivion awaits me, living a life that revolves only around me.
Old and tired, why are we still alive?
In this oblivion called tottering around on bones
That have begun their steady descent into the graveyard dirt.
Nears and dears congregate and commiserate wondering
When they will find relief from cleaning up your refuse;
And oblivion to us is death being a fog-dispelling beacon.

Insidious fear grips the mediocre heart churning the gut
Not born to make the grade of brilliant achievement.
School will be over and no longer will there be a place to hide.
Oblivion working somewhere, trying hard to appease a rather
common wife.

A cockroach lives for nine days after losing its head;
We must be evolved, for we aren't rioting.
On the frostiest night in many a year and
Stretch limousines can't guarantee respite from six-hour delays.

Sitting at my work desk one filthy summer afternoon,
I could be dead before my brain begins to know…
Some nutcase popped an ICBM eight minutes ago
Wonder what afterlife is, as we indulge in some late-night discourse.

I heard cull lists being drawn.
Was it for us humans or for the frightened cows?

The virus spreads like locusts and research has lost its fight.
The virus has got everybody's number except mine.
In ten years, all will be dead and the world will be mine.
What a miserable dream being the last one alive!
A solitary dinosaur in a cave, wondering why the sun disappeared;
Asteroids have no sensitivity for our wills of perpetuation
That we might disappear seems more fact to be than fiction.

We like to think otherwise resorting to prayer and theoretical science;
"Our intellect will survive!" we exclaim.
The benevolent God would never let us perish.
We are the chosen few, if anybody does exist, we do.
Of the same caliber in this cold forsaken Cosmos –
Asteroids have no particular sensitivities, will we perish
Before some debris floating in, obliterates us from outer space.

A mound of earth under a bell jar, where insects multiply wild;
That is this planet to a viewer from another universe.
Each sect fighting the other in the perception of servitude;
None wants a martyr's fate, each must have its pound of dust.

Spare a thought for the lover who cherishes his cross of fate;
The ultimate insight into the nature of life is not a coward's work.

Watch a foetus on a sonogram; spot the wildly pulsating chest;
Inconceivably tiny growing bundle of flesh.
Attachment starts in the mind and grows in the heart;
"Touch me not," says the blue-green boy as he turns his back.
Some births never come to pass; some kind of oblivion
To be left staring impotently at the wall.

"Don't step on my stump," says the fallen tree.
"They cut me down because the sunlight got blocked;
What about the oxygen I brought, how could they have forgot?
Don't step on my trunk because I don't hurt the way you want."

Under the dim street lights,
We relive all our loves gone by;
Under the dim street lights,
We wonder what happened over the years gone by.

In the twilight of our lives,
We know we will never know why;
Under the glow of the full moonlight,
Wish we had said our final goodbyes.

Oblivion Undone

Life is the pursuit of knowledge, both lived and learned.

Exaltation in the service of creation, humanity—the only God to know.

We have been heading for oblivion for a long time now.

If eternal life be our refuge,

This mad wantonness would lend for wisdom and maturity.

In some other life, somewhere else,

Be it another dimension or another birth.

Eternal life has always existed;

Its perception strongest when consciousness is unwaveringly constant.

There is no sleep and no need for dreams;

The presence of thought knows of its singularity and not.

Oblivion will grant a freedom from illusion and desire;

Oblivion will reinforce a kind of renunciation,

A staging ground for the illumination of the divine.

Realization is not a creation of the intellect.

Surrounded by books and talk, the best you can get

Is a pinched, holier-than-thou countenance.

Pretending to know all because you aren't really sure.

Look pious, act pious, and suffer silently in your own pretensions.

Hope for a transcendental vision of a non-ordinary state of mind.

A glimpse of that transcendental eternal that convinces
That oblivion is not a relevant phenomenon –
Only a transitory state of mind.

It's All in There

The pain and the pleasure last at most for a lifetime;
The beauty of a poem lasts forever.

Looking everywhere for some kind of meaning
To all those moments that can't be explained.
Alone, uncomfortable, solitude, looking odd—a misfit
People milling around, don't they look so engrossed?
Someone's in love, someone's being adored;
Some are just so beautiful—no one's missing out.

The grass is greener on the other side always.
What kind of happiness is felt by their thoughts?
Are you really suffering or is that only your mind –
Trying to assert its independence
Stuck in weird depths of subconscious dross?

The greatest asset you ever have is your own brain.
If you can use it to open, to make it a key in a lock –
Divine inspiration will follow.

And then, magic happens!
Just to be sitting here in Covent Garden,
Maybe, being born is worth it—a tenuous premise at the best of times.
There is a tedium of existence to endeavor.

So Free

Originality was when creation was manifested by divine power.
All else is old wine in new bottles.
Personal intent is discarded; divine intent is what forges the way.
There must be a reason for what the almighty wishes.

Light of head and young of heart,
Nothing to do with the physical state.
To be playful, optimistic, creative, open, and always looking ahead;
That is what it means to be young—energetic, not of body,
But of spirit and mind.

The ultimate is a personal experience
Not to be found through organized forms of devotion.
The direct experience, the shifting miasmas in the forehead,
There is no meaning to an individual existence.

A Perfect World?

Forget for a moment—clear your mind of all preconceptions.
Assume there is no need to practice openly a religion;
Assume there is a God everybody feels and nobody denies;
Or accepts there isn't—it's a personal choice.

What kind of nation would that be,
Where we have our thoughts privately but uphold the discipline,
By doing what is decidedly good for the collective
But the catch is the social inequity of wealth
Between the few and the most?

What does it mean to be rich, if achievement be the way of life?
Would we really care about lucre, save its purpose to balance?
Or as a tool and side-effect of some successful intellectual exercise,
I think we would settle for some simple life
As long as we were recognized in the way we like –
And that makes us feel loved and happy and satisfied.

Well, that makes communism sound like a people-wide spiritual exercise!
Replication of the perfect soul nation-wide—the yogi factory.
But the thing is that man is not perfect and hence will eventually rebel;
For, he needs his space and freedom and time to change.
Metamorphosis—shifting positions, shifting states of mind,
And settling into the eternal groove of his choice.

Democracy works for man is neither perfect nor a machine.

That is the nature of existence—let what is and what will, be.

Otherwise, wouldn't the maker have created a perfect world in the first place?

The Fabric of Developing Nations

Not the celebrity, the industrialist, or the film producer,
Not the artist, the painter, or the leader;
The fabric of a nation is the largest common mass.
Not the sportsman who gets paid so we can worship his glance,
Cheer for every victory that comes our way, criticize the loss,
Doping, drinking, dozing—our future plight somehow forgot.

The developing are not the ten percent English-speaking college crowd,
Nor the smug pretties giggling over some sanitary talks.
The developing I see are the poor urchins begging on the filthy streets,
And the obnoxious eunuchs being so because they are expected to be.

What a waste of time trying to educate the slums, breeding mouths!
The socio-economic system runs on a loaded gun—beyond repair.
These rich countries are becoming a latrine, on the streets and grounds.
The fabric of these nations is beggary thrust on the rural exodus to town.

You don't need a classroom to teach common sense;
You only need a head and heart to learn the patriotic alphabet.
Aghast at the swollen belly destitute with an already tattered brood,
These nations are paying the price for unsafe sex under a leaking roof.
The global village is here—the whole world will bear the weight.
The time for effects in isolation was left behind in the Middle Ages.

The smart bright girl paints a prostitute's plight—only a child!
"Do it for her, for us—be alive, live her pain, arise!"
Doing something, feeling saintly—a right earned, a guilt massaged:
I can't live the delusion that the road ahead is littered with
Foreign brands and bucks; the few don't make a country's consciousness.
Though I want to do—what, where and how I beg to ask?

Be

If divinity needed us not to enjoy being,
If Samsara was really this Machiavellian thing,
He/She/It wouldn't have created it!
Provided you believe he exists, or she if finicky,
In the natural order of things, the veil will drop.
But, be true, be here, and be now,
To feel what he means to you personally.

That great love and divinity,
Asserting itself, matter of subtlety.
And with a manifest world,
Evolving eventually to rocketry –
Love, celebration, bliss of different kinds,
At different levels,
The play of divinity, a great love.

The truth of monism is to make you aware.
Learn how to handle the pain,
Not to distract you from your ken.
That which is your destiny, fulfill your perception of existence.
Enjoy the present, just 'Be'; whatever is, needs no apology.

A different nature called 'truth' will be revealed.
Don't worry about the what and the why of divinity.

When the time is right, when you have played your part,
The ladder of life will show itself clear to sight.

If you get too hung up on idolatry,
You are never going to get beyond a child-like mentality.
Always dependent, always asking, always unsure—and somewhat guilty.
Learn to 'Be', feel the will of the singular divinity.

Malaise

Beneath and within the ocean concealed,
Myriad pretty and colourful beings.
Above the surface, limitless horizons and a beautiful sky.
A cool breeze touches your sleeve as you purvey a glimpse of paradise.

I am fine but you are not—only fools go looking for a perfect life.
"I am the greatest," he concludes—feels no love to get back in line.
He's a fat cat, Mr. Mack—feeling like he's got it all right.
Fly on man, in your delusion kite, you have an opinion and so have I.

If you reach Maha-nirvana, call yourself 'repaired'.
If you are free of karmic sickness, call yourself 'healed'.
When you have done enough, you will feel the futility
Of wallowing in shutter happiness and notching up your deeds.

Between you and me, between existing and not,
Call yourself repaired, live in keeping with the maker's wish.
Follow his every wish, his tear, his embrace, his desire for a kiss;
Feel his love that is a summation of everything; you are healed:

    Be healed, you will feel the malaise of those bequeath.
    The brothers and sisters in arms, how can you be well,
    When all is simply a divine wish!

The Cave of Brahma

Dancing musical deities waft across in ethereal clouds.
Everyone's laughing noiselessly at a splendid cosmic song.
Purity is the absence of malice, desire, and tarnishing grit.
Perfection is doing whatever it takes to abide by the maker's wish.

God loves you; God is your friend;
God is your well-wisher, constantly watching over your actions;
God is with you, God is you!
Never expecting reverence or hysteric exhibitions of swaying heads.

Give me no visions from the singular God.
I would rather learn from my father's talk.
Free from Malaise, Brahmananda waits with bated breath.
"Show me the answer," he says. "What was beneath the divine intent?"

The *Kalachakra* spins forever on.
From its whirring came the primal sound—'Jai Guru Dev!'
Always saying, "want you, want you to; know you, know yourself"
Om Namho Shivaya, you and I are enmeshed like a Boolean truth.

I am nobody's Guru; I am whatever you need to feel full.
Was the divine manifestation vanity?—He impassively blinks not,
Not a clue in those eyes piercing through the eternal point.
Will all questions vanish when consciousness enters the supreme void?

The Summit of Shiva

Went in search of the mother divine, found instead the fostering mind.
Went in search of eternal life, found in it a kind of suicide.
A magical tunnel emanates from forehead to her Kali form,
Life is a pilgrim's ken, guitar in hand and a song on the way to sing.

"Good morning! Beautiful young man," Babaji sitting on his plateau.
"Look at me, look at you, look at what you can become:
Father—threat, superior, better, the idiot son, me happy you not;
Mother—seeing him in a way that fulfils your desires, is he a toy?
Elder—lightening rod, bending my back, taking all my flak;
Dislike—you don't like yourself, that which you carry inside;
No escape—afraid of what people are going to say, needing them;
Sniffing—asking you out, you have an exquisite effect on my mind.
Surreal, ephemeral, incredible sadness and joy;
Poignant extremes, a sharpness of being not ordinarily found;
Clarify—can't control your sensitivities, that's why you want to know;
Privilege—dispensing favors, let go of your self-esteem, be lucky;
Love—don't look for dignity or apology; don't miss the moment;
Silence—the end of seeing whatever and whichever way convenient."

"Who am I?" The brilliant white light, the melodic beauty of sound.
The unfettered expanse of thought, the stillness of the supreme void.

Walking Through a Nuclear Wasteland Called Earth

Always better to be at ground zero—wouldn't feel the moment of death;
Not suffering the world war that is certain to cover all parts of Earth.
The island an hour away will bear the brunt.
Don't they look so happy? Nuclear exchanges aren't really their problem!
The next generation will all be Mongoloids, mutant ninja turtles!
More likely will be a lingering torturous death by contamination.
Intensely hurting spores and liquid bowels, polluted air, food, and water,
Everyone can stand around and watch the mass suicides; what a sight!

When all are gone, the financial hub that was once will crumble.
The entire world will feel the impact, homeless people—bankrupt.
Civil riots, wars everywhere, nations fighting over a loaf of bread.
The jungle is no longer here and there,
Human animals are everywhere—going on for a thousand years.
All that evolution we went through, what a complete waste!

With great intellect comes great responsibility.
Was he the father of modern science or the biggest enemy of mankind?
Ghosts everywhere holding astral children tightly to chest,
Walking around thinking why we turned our progeny to dust.
Emerging from the cave of Bramha after penance isn't going to help;
I am walking through our legacy—this nuclear wasteland called Earth.

No Emotional Baggage

But for symmetry,
I would never have known if
Sky met Earth or otherwise.

The lords laugh at webs
Beaded with dewdrops and rain;
A singular fool stumbles when he first learns to walk.

Towers of stone paint,
Moonlight on walls in streets of cobblestone,
Dance as dead in churches wearing ears of poppy,
Then drop as dead when your partner leaves you alone by the steps.

A luminescent God hidden,
Fading then you see the straw.
Wonder why he ever made:

    Surreal dreams hushed me to sleep.
    Fragile wounds tender tears well within.
    Even scars open to;
    Time ticks lightly by.

    They are grown.
    The last lunch is on.
    Tomorrow, they will be gone.

Though deep was my loving,

The mist swirling beyond my allowed desire.

Brittle dust strewn in a thousand greens,

Only unrequited beautiful love do men and women excruciatingly write.

Read with a flowing heart,

The lines that stretch across the pages yellow and white.

Aged with time, aged with pain, an age too late to remember or hate.

Homecoming

The stillness of a night, the conception of a child,
The wee hours before dawn, a baby is born.
The first light of day, the awareness of sight,
The bustle of noon, the teachers in school,
The early evening, the flush of youth,
The onset of age, the coming of dusk,
The stillness of night, the inertness of death,
The wee hours before dawn, the final rites by a funeral pyre.

My God, the Golden Child

All those legends they drill into your head
About warriors bronzed and muscled and dyed in the bluest black.
Many arms, many weapons, sometimes many heads,
Rescuing lands and the hapless and sometimes a princess:

Those are the Gods we believe;
The Gods we imagine and build in our heads.

That was the vision I was on the lookout for –
Macho and brave and untouchable beyond the realms of doubt.
When it came, it was exactly how I wished it to be—quite unexpected;
That made it real beyond the wildest paranormal experience.

Then there he was, sitting on the floor,
The golden child at the center of a golden glow.
Two nascent teeth grinning through curly folds,
He reaches out to you and you lose all that you hold close:

You lose all hate and anger and general angst,
He needs his mother and you are glad that it is you he wants.

The embodiment of all in a creative universe;
The innocence of purpose and optimism you behold;
Unconditional love and role models interchanged;
A fulfillment found in love that measures no scale.

Happiness is being as happy as can be.

Happiness is being happy with your destiny.

And the child that you carry within,

Happiness is being happy with God eventually.

Whoever he might be,

Happiness is finding a love that makes life an enchanted wish!

It

Is 'it' you or is 'it' me?
Is 'it' some Johnny waiting under a Christmas tree?
For a kiss and a chance to see…
Is 'it' a Sally waiting for an opportunity to marry someone neat?

Is 'it' the Universe and the heavens we cannot see?
Is 'it' the light that traveled the black void seeking our sight?
Is 'it' the circle that brings my actions back to my side?
Is 'it' the infinite that defies measure and always baffles our minds?

Is 'it' the haughty girl who thinks she is it?
Is 'it' her ego that shadows her every belief?
Is 'it' the hurt that she leaves trailing her feet?
Is 'it' a trance that her beauty flaunts?

Is 'it' a love that you think is a summation of me?
Is 'it' a state of grace that never was conceived?
Is 'it' a benediction of destiny and the wish of a will?
Is 'it' that unseen puppeteer who makes us frantic by the strumming of his strings?

My Poet's Pen

Oblivion is a good place to be.
If you are a poet, you'll get there for free!
Nowadays, no one reads this stuff, laddie;
It's grooving bodies on fantasy TV that feed the babies:

> You probably asked them for money,
> You'll be lucky if they don't ask you for any.

Showed him the first, thinking he was something else.
He thought I was in depression and went running for help:

> How could I tell him,
> How would he ever understand,
> That I reached greater heights
> When wracked by despair?

We get no respect from this friggin' community.
We gotta keep ourselves flying in the face of adversity.
Found a room and leased it for a week or two.
The copper thought we were subversives from a cultist group:

> We get no respect from this friggin' community.
> The copper wanted to get his kiddies through university.
> We gotta settle the man if we wanna make our moves.
> We didn't, so he cancelled our license to think politically.

The poet's domain lies in the land.
Tread in parallel with unfolding life.
As each step grows firmer and surer,
The pen slithers across faster and smoother.

Tried to be witty but they thought I was silly;
I knew I was lazy but they thought I was crazy;
Went to church and tried very hard to pray;
They thought I was Christian but aren't we all simply humans in some higher place!

To Cross O'er the Seas

There's a lil' office,
An oven as hot as cold;
To this lil' office I often go,
With a lil' black book of my own.

They split up the Earth,
So that became theirs and this became ours.
Now I go to a lil' office first,
So they would let me get past their door.

They called for a convention of heads;
Everyone spoke of governance and common sense:

    We got more and they got less;
    Let them starve and we'll feed the rest.
    They ain't ours and growing too fast to care;
    We ain't gonna go down for the poor someplace else.

I took a trip down to this very special place.
The lady took a closer look at my fuzzy face,
Then wrinkled her pretty nose,
And rather sharply spoke:

    "So, kind Sir, why to our land have you deemed to travel?"
    She wanted an answer but I had to race.

"Well lady! What's yours and what's mine
Ain't the Earth bequeathed to us all"

I really shouldn't have, you know,
All I got was a reddish mark.
Now I go to a lil' office first
Collecting as I go, many, many red marks more.

The Whispering Wind

Seeing the whispering wind and knowing she was in the ocean moods,
I listened to her words and learned of many a happening:

> Choo shew choo shew, cool, cool gathering chutes,
> Hoo hoo blowing fumes, faster, faster swirling fondues,
> Fair and blond, moving gently in the prairie blooms,
> Faster, faster in the air, quick, quick get away from here!

Ancient tales from distant lands,
I listen all day to stories of many kinds.
There is one on whom she is especially soft,
She tells me of him cooing passionately by my side:

> "It is the true brave
> Who go to battle without their swords."

The crops are aflame, the cane fields are burning bright.
Hustling around, she fans the fires I just put out.
"Go away!" I say, she laughs and turns to those that survived.
Covered in ash and incensed by heat, I demand a reply:

> Amused at my indignant stare, she gustily clarifies,
> "There is always a price you cannot avoid.
> You forget so easily but I don't, so I'll come again tomorrow,
> The end is a beginning when you accept the sorrows you beget."

A letter arrived one day, as I sat reading by the porch.
She slipped up unbidden and blew away the smoke:

> Summon your bugles, blow your trumpets,
> The last bastion of innocence has fallen!
> Contentment, that ethereal mist
> Is my utopia forever lost in its haze!

"Enough of that, boy. Now, do you have a message for your girl to be?"
So, I gave her one knowing it would soon be heard:

> Beloved to come, what would I give thee?
> What better than these diamonds of the night?
> *Je* regret these are much beyond my means,
> You would have to settle for my poor love instead.

He holds a vow of silence but one day that broke.
So, I stopped rustling the leaves
And gathering my billowing skirts,
Sat beside and waited for him to speak:

> I kept peeling off the skins.
> For every one found, there were hundreds in between.
> Reduced to a vain pursuit, this could go on unceasing.
> The only way out is that which comes unasked and unseen.

Bewildered, I frown but she's a few steps in front.
"If death is a game, why does it frighten?
If death is an illusion, why does its inertness chill?"
She tousles my locks fondly and tries to assure:

> "In time to come,
> All your questions will be satisfactorily realised!"

The Land of More Suns Than One

And then suddenly I was catapulted out of my sleep,
Into a land in which it seemed the sun never set.
Robbed of the softness of bed and the comfort of warmth,
The bile rose in protest against the panicking breast:

> "Where was I, how did I get here?
> Why me, only me, nobody but me, it couldn't be me!"

The mind struggled with the perception of what it saw.
The noisy streets, the sound of children in the deep,
The filthy air, the cleansing breeze, the still of the night.
How did I get here? This was not the Earth I believed:

> Who could I blame? Pinch the flesh and see!
> Oh! It hurts real, and I am not dreaming in my dreams!

When the rationale tires and reason gives up its tricks,
The conscious finally accepts and falls asleep, tired:

> Shade by a solitary bush in the land of more suns than one,
> When I awoke, I thought all would be well;
> I would be back in my own bed and snoring like a pig;
> I would awake and laugh, the nightmare a release from beneath.

I opened my eyes and the sun lay suspended still beyond.
Not a dream but I wanted not the sanctity of the make-believe.
In a growing disease of burning skin,
I found the profoundness of this land
That was hitherto so well concealed.

I walked on and on, on the old road straight,
The furnace turned the day into a daze.
It was a desert of stone, all white but shining light.
The sky was white too, not blue but a mellowing hue:

Blisters came and went, then came on top again.
Blood flowed from my feet but I stopped for nothing.
The sight was fading from my eye and I thought I might be dying.
In resignation, I found a peace; I knew what was happening.

At a distance far, I saw him approach;
A great white beard and a full white robe.
Too far still but I heard a voice—in my head, not my ear.
Don't ask me why, you are here because you wanted to be:

Don't ask, you are here because you wanted to be.
Don't act stupid because you are expected to be.

He was not and then he was—he was standing there.
I fell to my knees, it seemed the right thing to supplicate:

"Oh, great one! What land is this?" I asked.
"This is the land of truth, a land where nothing survives."
"Then oh, white one! This is now my home,
For, nowhere else shall I go!"

Some eyes can never go blind.
This is my home, for, where else is there to go now?

The Cosy Cushion of Bliss

Happiness is a five-hundred CC motorbike kicked into a pulsing roar,
Chatting and drifting in strong sunshine on a blistering afternoon:

> Sitting at the neighbors' and the lights go out;
> Singing a song while it's dark and all distraught.
> Then the moments pass and the candles are lit;
> Could sense our harmonizing souls only when the eyes were drawn.

Just love this longing for the cosy cushion of bliss;
When it comes, it will; when she decides to descend, she will.

Half of life was lost in thinking the what;
When it was time to be doing, we were sleeping dogs:

> He's got a bronze cross around his neck.
> Ask if it's fashion, common sense, or something else.
> Says none of that but mother believes in the saint.
> That's fine boy, carry on with what you got in your hands.

Just love this longing for the cosy cushion of bliss;
When it comes, it will; when she decides to descend, she will.

Can't stay in the city, gotta follow the advice of the mighty.
Can't stay in the city, gotta follow the scent of opportunity.

Just love this longing for the cosy cushion of bliss;
When it comes, it will; when she decides to descend, she will.

It's Christmas and the bands are vying for a rating in the game.
It's Christmas and most think it's time to be prancing again:

> After much and too much, can no longer be sure.
> I captured a mood in 'the feeling of loss'.
> The flow of words, the chorus of thoughts,
> Can't feel a thing,
> Don't know a thing,
> Don't want to know what it means.

Just love this longing for the cosy cushion of bliss;
When it comes, it will; when she decides to descend, she will.

I know she will,
I can feel she will,
She will, she will,
One day, she suddenly will.

A Common Lot

A husband who's forgotten he's still one;
What choice had she but an ungainly one.
She's looking into a well and considering a jump;
It all started when she began listening to herself.

The inner voice is the wisest of all,
The wisest is never very pleasant at all.

She grew into youth under a misguiding hand.
To be loved was to be always heard;
To find elusive love she persevered;
To every whim she thoroughly indulged:

How can pain be shorn from existence?
Temporary happiness lasts only a second.
Reality was to convenience warped;
She was trapped in an inert situation.

He would be her life,
The reason for her being,
She ignored the unsettling feeling;
It was her voice within screaming a warning.

The safe past receded fast;
The dread of an unknown future lay in front.

Living vicariously doesn't count for much;
Battles are fought and won mostly on foot:

> She had a second child;
> She learned from the first and amended the present.

What mother would call her work a chore?
Allow the jingle of gilt-edged coins to change her goal.
Can you settle her penance by slivers of notes?
What if nature too asked for her due tomorrow:

> Play a fostering role and see the intricacies unfold.
> Perhaps, you might be ready then to talk less than you know.

They became adults and went their separate ways.
Watching them gave her the belief she too would, one day.
No longer was she frightened by a new dawn;
She was beginning to make her time count:

> She is not a woman, mother, or wife;
> She forges exactly what she likes.
> She has understood the shortness of time;
> She is flying gloriously into the sunset of life.

Worried Forever

You are born premature and they are worried you will die;
You make it through the night and they are worrying about tonight.
The medical man says, "You must beware for a year;
He's a premature child and might not last the fortnight."

You can trade in the worry and settle for the grief;
You can trade in the grief and settle for some peace.

You are old enough and they send you to school;
Before too soon, they are worrying if you can play the flute.
You never did but they kept worrying anyway;
Something serious was amiss and they should have known straight away.

You can trade in the worry and settle for the grief;
You can trade in the grief and settle for some peace.

You get a fever and they think it's an epidemic;
It isn't but they worry for the worst and barely sleep a wink.
Then you recover and go playing some sport;
You get hit on the head and they worry you might turn out stupid.

You can trade in the worry and settle for the grief;
You can trade in the grief and settle for some peace.

You are a big boy and the serious years are here;
They worry that you might be not be burning the oil enough.
You will never make a professional at this rate, boy!
Get your head out of trivial pursuits before it's too late.

If you can't do what you want, why even exist?
If you can't handle the weight, go hang yourself somewhere else!

You make it past and the next step on the ladder awaits;
You get even that and they are worrying about your grades.
And food and money and your careless inconsiderate ways;
You graduate and they are worrying about all that lies ahead.

If you are lucky, you won't be indoctrinated;
If you got the sense, you won't keep the faith;
If you got a handle on yourself, you won't go wrong;
Don't settle for some God because you have learned to fear.

You can trade in the worry and settle for the grief;
You can trade in the grief and settle for some peace.
You love worrying because you don't have to live;
You don't have a life and worrying fills in for bliss.

Dedicated To

Dedicated to my Guru,
From whom I learned everything I know.
Dedicated to my Guru,
From whom I learned the value of words.
Dedicated to my Guru,
From whom I learned to keep my silence.
Dedicated to my Guru,
He knows everything there is to know.

Dedicated to my Guru,
Who taught me unconditional love.
Dedicated to my Guru,
Who taught me how to suffer.
Dedicated to my Guru,
From whom I learned the patience to observe.
The patience to endure;
The patience to love;
The patience to sit by a garden window;
The patience to let go.

Dedicated to my Guru,
He's the greatest Guru in the universe.
Jai Guru Maharaj!
Jai Gurudev!

The Pattern of Sound

The tiny drops that splash in a puddle;
Can you hear the rhythm, sitting by the hole?

    That was an orchestration of plastic and string;
    The mind nudges reverently saying, "Look for the cadence!"
    The lilt was a sequence and then confluent;
    It was poetry in sound, for such I was told.

It is a structure of flesh and bone;
Call it an ear but it sees the notes.
Symbols flash in frames before the hidden eye;
Arising as they did from differing pitches and twangs:

    The rains have refrained to a faint drizzle;
    Nature's symphony now reduced to sporadic whistles.

The interval had changed and the tempo left;
The heavens might pour to a primal dance again.
Then there shall be a beat and a swaying motion;
The pattern of sound shall reverberate for an eternity again:

    Cascades of compositions, surmounted by words;
    Then of poetry, now it's a song.

What was the dialect, what was the content?
What can I say but I haven't a clue!
The tones gathered together and leapt for heart;
The planet had changed but the chords were the same:

> The lines of blending chords and bars,
> Faster and faster they descended into a tasteless jumble.

That symphony of sounds,
Unheard by the human soul, heard only by the lords.
Of what nature are those reverberations and scales?
They say meditate in a void to partake heaven's dictates:

> Did you meet the commonest of man?
> He said music is the expression of emotions felt.

In each, to find a song of its own.
So, I said of all those feelings we hold,
The pattern of sounds so much in fact,
Streams of thoughts and the colors that arose:

> The market has a singular taste,
> We all move together in unwitting step.

Steady State

All of life sometimes feels like buying time;
Mostly spent in a waiting line.
Waiting for love, waiting for respect,
Waiting for failure, and waiting to rise in courage.
Till you search for a freedom of being,
Rather than a recklessly contemplated end.

From cradle to grave, we are victims of expectations.
Those of the parents, those of extended association,
Those of professional ties, and those of general human condition.
From work to leisure, expectation dogs our every step with relentless determination.

The standards to be met, be it home, spouse, or the clothes you wear;
The chains seem to be everywhere and every breath becomes a conscious effort.
From waking up in the morning to dragging yourself through each passing moment,
You crave for an end, which is hardly the way out of these plunging depths.

And in the middle of all these sentiments,
Comes the magical moment—a chance to break free of all your little entanglements.
Time slips by and the gates are closing but who cares?

For a moment, you are your own man,
And that is a priceless reaffirmation of independence.

As you sit at your worker's desk and the pressure starts mounting,
All the various figures of authority demand your best in urgent behest.
As you single-mindedly blunder through the corridors of endeavor,
You find a steady state that is akin to a deep state of reflection and introspection.

So quite accidently comes our way, the jewel we seek in constant earnest.
You don't need to be in lotus position,
Or run away to a secret asylum in total renunciation.
The center within is the place to be,
The ultimate freedom in the middle of all the ferment.

The steady state of detached doing,
The steady state of detached being,
Eventually brings the liberation that we seek and rarely find.
Seated in the middle, the world spins around, inconsequentially and immaterially,
Like distant sounds in the street, heard from the rooftops of towering mountains.

Inspiration

Inspiration is a wonderful thing
To be found in a look,
Or the nuance of a face,
Or the riveting flow of gentle words.

Ecstasy is an uplifting feeling.
It can bring one out from the pits of despair;
It can be found in the gurgling laughter of a child,
Or the soft patter of little feet on wooden floors.

Whatever it may be,
It comes from an all-abiding love
That embraces all
And brings life a golden glow.

You can sing a thousand songs,
Or write a million words.
But it takes only a little love,
To make your world whole!

"Dream Baby"

We asked Almighty God for a bonny child.
We got more than we realized.
Twice more over than what we dreamed at night.

The leaves are falling from the Ginkgo trees,
And Hibiya is teeming with professional ties;
I am thinking of my dream baby's innocent cries.

The flight from Narita is not far away;
Soon, I shall be united with the essence of our lives;
Holding him in my arms and rocking him goodnight.

Mother says dream baby misses me.
I think of him at Sengakuji when tired,
And homecoming seems ever so sweet this time.

There is snow in the air.
Christmas bells will be ringing in many homes.
I realize that wherever he is, that is the place for me to be.

Musings on a *Dimanche Parisien*

I look for Mona Lisas in real life;

Not dead women in old paintings

Hanging on Louvre walls smiling benignly at passers-by.

Paying a few francs to feel special—cultured, erudite, and intellectually bright;

Or maybe, to kill time and loneliness and no other reason why.

But had these passers-by not existed,

What motivation would have driven the artist or the man of science?

But perhaps at some higher plane,

They did it all on someone's insistence.

And in doing so, no longer felt that they did anything at all!

And so, I might well be wrong;

For, the admiration might not be a cynics fodder,

But a genuine appreciation of mankind's knowledge and its struggles.

I quest for *ma liberte* –

From work, life, regulations, and ties.

But like vibrant colours in summer blossoms,

My sons remind me that surely, they can't be bondages.

Of course not! They are the delight of what could otherwise be a miserable life.

Maybe that's why we are here to celebrate these ties.

The enlightened man goes nowhere.

Reduces suffering or contributes to the evolution of mankind,

By creating his own moments or those for others.

Works of genius, a statement of everyone's life;

And not just a need to be special,

But at some higher place,

Serving as a vessel for the almighty radiance to channel.

The Flame (A Song)

The flame of joy,
The flame of pain,
The flame of being,
The flame of life.
Burns always
In our hearts,
In our minds,
The reason
To be.

Love the flame,
Love the flame,
Feed the flame,
The rise and fall of *Om*.
In the flame,
Constantly…
That's all
We seek.

I am Everywhere (A Song)

I am everywhere.   [G]
I am in the spin of the Earth;   [C/IIIrd pos]
I am in the cries of the children,   [G]
As mother cooks them supper.   [C]
I am in the fire of the winter,   [G]
That warms the dweller in the rubble.   [C]
I am with the dead soul,   [G]
Who wonders why the mourners   [C]
Grieve over his departure.   [G]

I am everywhere.
[G] [D...]
I am in the impersonal love   [C]
That binds us all together.   [G]
I am with the despairing parents,   [G]
"Why do our children hurt us so?" [C]
I am with the wizened children,   [C]
Their suffering was a comedy of errors. [G]

I am everywhere.   [G]
I am in the flame,   [C]
I am everywhere.   [G]

The Guru

They flocked to him by his door,
In the terrible heat and in the torrential downpour.
He was a guiding light for the teeming hordes,
The embodiment of all that in a fostering universe:

    The ripples through his tranquil being of concern to all,
    He became impatient and nervous like the rest of the lot.

Beaten by the harsh summer, the river dried to a trickle;
Beaten by the harsh summer, the old man was losing the battle.
One day, he came and sat by the banks of the river,
And a sparrow came to him.

She loved him dearly and could abide not in silence.
Perched on his shoulder, she beseeched him for an answer:

    Shed of all snares that entrapped and enslaved
    Of all desires that besot and were laid to rest,
    There is one that besots and will never leave unwept.
    My son, to him I bequeath the most precious of my possessions.
    Tell me, little one, why does he not come?
    My weary spirit desires to return.

The birds and beasts huddled in their commune,
The sparrow explained the cause of the troubles.

All grew pensive in recognition of the cycle;
Life without the Guru was unthinkable.
The blind old crow spoke as the pall grew unbearable:

> By the first curtains of the monsoon showers,
> The rising waters will bring him that which he most desires.

The river grew stronger, yet he sat half submerged.
One day, he saw something floating on a log downstream.
In saving the youth was the prophecy fulfilled,
He had found his son and his serenity was returning.

There is a symmetry in nature for those who believe in fate.
The like find the right and the right prove them sane.
In silence and in words, by day and sleeping night,
Surely and steadily went the Guru preserving the flame:

> Then the passage was complete and the son was cast alike.
> The old man took to his death bed and waited for respite.

The passing was in dignity as befits a man of the lord.
The mortal coil was laid to rest in a burning fire.
The mourning was a rejoicing, for they had an heir;
The mourning was a rejoicing, for he was a higher self:

> The youth settled into the void left behind;
> He was the custodian now of enlightened thought.

Seasons went by and a stick aided him walk.
Long grew his white beard and wavering was his walk.
One day, he came and sat by the banks of the river,
And a sparrow came to him.

PART III –
STARTING IN THE UK

Free Association

On the last day, Tara manifested her divine radiance
By giving me something in a way that cannot be understood.
You have nothing but you have me; be inspired, son.
Then, down—overwhelmed by this profound and inexplicable grace,
There was fear, uncertainty, and doubt, my mind is no longer my own.
Must be teenage hormones and social angst, being no longer sure.
Yet, what is this strange contentment that cannot be understood?

Then the realization—pain is from ignorance born;
Pain breaks the shackles, makes for a sensitive mind.
The start of the journey towards enlightened sight;
Feel it, abide it, trust it and write it.
Create and contribute,
By contemplating the way of all life with fellow sentient forms.

Suffering is the essence of life, the immersion in Advaita Vedanta.
The greatest love of your life is you yourself, the 'I'—all inside.
It is not about forgiving yourself but about loving yourself.
Enriching life experiences—not good intentions but good results.
Be the best you can be in the way you want to be:
You, who are that infinitesimal point that cannot be further divided.
Bring on the suffering, so may come forth the greatness of mankind.
For, that is the will of God—though I don't know why.

You and I (A Song)

[B7, B7, A, A, E Strum]

[Guitar Melody 1] When I hear your voice, honey,
[Guitar Melody 2] I cry joyfully.
[Guitar Melody 1] You will be there,
[Guitar Melody 1] When I see.

[E Strum, E Strum]

Live with me, die with me,
Love with me, hurt with me,
But never leave me;
I could never sleep.

[Guitar Melody 3] When I see your face, honey,
[Guitar Melody 4] I cry silently.
[Guitar Melody 5] You are not a weapon;
[Guitar Melody 6] You will be there,
[Guitar Melody 7] When I need.

Live with me, die with me,
Learn with me, grow with me,
But never leave me;
I could never weep.

[Guitar Melody 3] When I think of you, honey,

[Guitar Melody 4] What a way to be!

[Guitar Melody 5] You are not a weapon.

[Guitar Melody 6] You and I,

[Guitar Melody 7] Were meant to be.

[E Strum]

Illusion Revisited Today

What if you get stuck in an elevator and the lights go off?
You might attain Nirvana if nobody comes to get you.
Could have been describing life, you know!
Like the girl you love having a laugh at you saying, "what a fool, you!"

Maya is the start of dualism, the start of illusion;
The start of subtle warfare and hate, of sin and spirituality.
Man against woman, religion against race, friend against foe –
Imagine a dichotomy and there is a fight,
Frog against snake, Madrid against United.

Need keeps us glued, safe from ourselves;
Until evolution begins.
The realization that this is not serenity;
Now, the true nature of man can assert and revert.

Surmounting barriers, achievements great and small;
The realization of the deepest realization of loss, love.
And finally, the value of, the beauty of love that passes possessing,
Beyond the pure consciousness of the supreme void,
The translucent yellowish flakes of soft white love that emanate
From a divine being that does have a form.

But there are answers, that which are here and now.
How do you explain the miserable mangy dog scratching itself to death?
Or the poor unfed orphans that host a multitude of disease,
While your child plays merrily on the pretty lawns and mossy walls?

Don't give me the Karma story, Guru Dev!
Divine manifestation seems like vanity to me.
When I see the unbearable pain of the tortured body,
I wonder what is to be said of the doer and the sufferer,
Being one and the same.

Just Right, Sir

Ouch! A wee too hot, perhaps!
A lil' water would do well.
Ah! Perfect! How very pleasant!
Dear mind, deadly foe at times.
This is the way I wanna be,
Just right, Sir!

A spectator is all I wanna be;
An actor has to play his part.
All I have and all I want,
Not for me but for all around.

I can't say for sure if I am any wiser,
But I do know a little more:

    I can cry for the painter deserted by his muse;
    I can cry for the hapless pure;
    Then when the minstrel strums her harp,
    I find myself atop the plateaus of ecstatic thought.

    It churns my being to see the old in fading health.
    Nervous wrecks in fear of death;
    Reminded at every step,
    That mercy is fast-vanishing gold.

Yet they ask me how,
In this state, I am content.
So, I shall answer as I did.
A different place but it could well be the same:

> She offers me wine,
> Then says, "It's the best in the land."
> I turn it down point blank.
> "You ain't a connoisseur then," she exclaims.
> "No lady, not that kind;
> Connoisseur I am, but of human emotion alone!"

Sweet child of pattering feet and lilting voice,
There are lines on my face,
And my hairs are turning white.
Little girl of the lilting voice,
You remind me of a more innocent me.

I sit and stare outta the garden window;
It's raining and there's a chill in the air.
I get a sweater and it's pretty warm;
But it's only a sweater, not my lover's arms.

The skies o'er England are clear.
Oh! Land of lion hearts!
Your kings are all gone;
All that remains are these little lawns.

There's a bullet in my gun;
Once fired, I will be done.
I'll take off my belt,
Never ever to wear it again.

I met a man who spoke for a while,
He said he was waiting for the light:

'To understand is to forgive;
Benevolence is always compassionate.
Compassion loves all,
And to love is to be forever free.'

That's a great place to be.
Who knows what tomorrow's plans are?
As for now, this is the way he wants to be.
Just right, Sir!

Premonition of Death

Having a nice drink in the bar when the feeling began.
Turned to brother Andrew and said we got to leave:

    A short drive to Devereux Road but stopping on the way;
    It's a winter's night and the fog is starting to fade.
    He needs a charge and fits his wire to our car;
    I am dislocating and that's only the start.

Hurried into my flat and finished stashing his car;
The keyboard is in the back and the VCR is on the way.
Dragged across my gear and said, "Don't touch the bats!"
Said goodnight rushing in and went straight into the bath:

    I am reducing the pressure and the pulse is slowing down;
    I am building up courage for something about to turn me around.

Waiting and coping and then she came out of nowhere;
Don't know if it was her but they are all the same anyway.
The force stood in front and I could feel its gaze;
"Look at me and concentrate," it said:

    It didn't need to say, for there was It and only It;
    I was locked in a trance and could think of nothing, save It.

It started at eleven and went on till one;
Then It left as abruptly as It had come.
I got five minutes to fathom what had happened;
Before the premonition of death began to settle:

> I am about to die in the worst possible way;
> I will be killed by the state after being tortured to death.

It got worse and I called brother Andrew at home;
Told him what had happened and asked him to come over.
He said, "It's late and you got to get some rest."
I said, "My time is up and I would be joining the dead":

> Called the master but he was somewhere away.
> Spoke to his son and said, "Calm me down, I am so scared!"
> Kept down the phone but my pulse started to race;
> My heart was gonna explode as I went off to bed.

Flitted in and out of restful daze, then came awake again;
The force is back but as a circle instead.
It opens as a cut in space and compels me to cross;
I am leaving my flesh but the mind says, "May be not!"
We are locked in a struggle and I impose my will:

> Everything is gone and I am alone with my fears;
> I got too many things undone, it can't be my turn yet.

The master's back and blames my diet;
I say, "They are coming to finish me off tonight."
He says, "Eat your bread and don't stay awake."
I ask him if I should kill myself and he says, "Do what you like":

> Went to the neighbors, couldn't ask for help;
> Came out looking insane and prepared myself for death.

Its dawn and I am still alive.
Went over to the landlord's and told him my tale;
I heard voices outside that were trying to intimidate.
I am an innocent man, I didn't say what I meant:

> He is kind and tries to soothe.
> How can I explain the potency of the pull?
> I come out and he says, "Go to the countryside."
> I didn't say, "I don't think you understand my plight."

The sirens are blaring and they could be coming for me;
Phoned JP and asked him how long I would be free.
He said, "Don't worry, you will be around till sixty-five;
I can't come over, I got a bad back."

> The upstairs guy is cleaning his flat;
> I don't think it's for the girl he's about to entertain.

The subliminal messages from 'the mad one' began.
The people thought she was divine;
She had become the ruler of the land;
She had much to avenge, now that she was mad:

> My abused bride would be over with her spies;
> She would shoot me for the dishonor she felt in her mind.
> I had a minute to ponder the choice;
> I had a minute to commit suicide.

Got up and took a ride to the airport;
Saw pity reflected for me in everybody's eyes.
Is there a tacit arrangement that I shall die by my master's side?
Am I taking the flight back to be a bird in a cage?:

> I heard voices about cull lists being drawn;
> Was it for us humans or for the frightened cows?

Got back to my hometown and thought there was a chance;
Walked out of the door waiting for the hit squad to arrive.
He had assured that I would live for as long as I want;
Did that mean he would convince me to top myself for the common
God?:

The entire world believed we were man and wife;
A medium gleaned from her that she had dreamed of me one night.
She went around saying I had an affair with her in school;
Was I hallucinating, or was she, or did she think that was true?

You are '*marsayfe*', so you cannot die;
But you have to, so the world can forget the lie.
She got your money and blew it up on her loves;
She's been getting around because you never went to her.
She was denied her rights and that drove her to spite;
Now we know that you were never told why.

They told everyone but you,
And you thought you were unlucky in love.
You lost years when you already had it all;
All you had to do was go to her but you didn't know.

You gotta die so the world can forget a double crime;
You gotta die so you are not the last one left alive.
There is another way—we can declare you insane;
In time to come, the world could adapt to yet another feint.

I don't think you wanna be shut in the aquarium of duds;
There is only sedation and you will never get to walk.
The screaming goes on all night and stops only at dawn;
I am sending a pill tonight, take it at nine.

The boy came over with the pill but I kept it on the sill;
Then at ten, my courage was built.
Death would be swift;
I ordered a feast and ate my final meal.

I took the capsule,
Watched the hands trace for over a minute.
In the constant fear of death,
Came to enjoy cheating it now and again.

I would come back and never find her waiting;
After a month, I gave up and thought it was never real:

It's a year past 2000 and I have fallen ill;
The premonition of death bells has been ringing again.
Called my master and asked if this would ever end;
He said it's a signal of caution, not dangerous intent.

The River Flows on Its Way (In the Year of Forgiving Yourself)

<table>
<tr><td>The river flows on its way,</td><td>[A]</td></tr>
<tr><td>As you sit and stare.</td><td>[E]</td></tr>
<tr><td>The swans start to fade away,</td><td>[A]</td></tr>
<tr><td>White as the snow that falls silently,</td><td>[D]</td></tr>
<tr><td>Gracefully they waltz away.</td><td>[A]</td></tr>
</table>

<table>
<tr><td>The Thames flows on its way,</td><td>[A]</td></tr>
<tr><td>The girls decline to stay in the shade.</td><td>[E]</td></tr>
<tr><td>Golden hair glistens by the morning sun,</td><td>[A, D]</td></tr>
<tr><td>Vivaciously they smile away.</td><td>[E]</td></tr>
</table>

<table>
<tr><td>Why don't we realize</td><td>[A]</td></tr>
<tr><td>What we mean to each other,</td><td>[E]</td></tr>
<tr><td>Before</td><td>[D]</td></tr>
<tr><td>It's too late?</td><td>[A]</td></tr>
<tr><td>If only we had followed our hearts,</td><td>[D]</td></tr>
<tr><td>There would be no sorrow</td><td>[E]</td></tr>
<tr><td>Today</td><td>[A]</td></tr>
<tr><td>As the river flows away.</td><td>[D]</td></tr>
</table>

The river flows on its way,   [A]
Bright as the stars that shine cheerfully. [D]
Faithfully,   [A]
We fade away.   [E]

Advaita Proposes

If X be the most oppressed person on Earth,
The question is –
Should X destroy the human race,
Because he suffers the most?
Or should he be happy for others,
And participate in their celebration of consciousness and life?

Science breeds superior weapons of death and destruction,
Sending rockets and signals into space, looking for similar things.
What if they turn out hostile and come marauding over here,
Turning movies into reality?
What demarcates progress from self-initiated extinction?

Imagine an ICBM launched eight minutes ago;
We die before we even begin to realize the futility of our life.
A nuclear or biological interlude quite terminally interrupt us;
Will be the epitaph nobody is left to recite for us.

That is the question Advaita proposes.
For, all is one is what they say.
Strive for that which you always have.
The capacity to submit, not deny—acceptance of your state of mind.
The first step towards the outstretched arms of divinity
And an eternal bliss nobody can take away from you.